fresh

NEW VEGETARIAN AND VEGAN RECIPES FROM FRESH RESTAURANTS

jennifer**houston**
ruth**tal**

Collins

An Imprint of HarperCollinsPublishers

Published by Collins, an imprint of HarperCollins Publishers Ltd.

Originally published by John Wiley & Sons Canada, Ltd.,
in both print and EPub editions: 2011

First published by Collins in this trade paperback edition and in an EPub edition: 2013

HarperCollins books may be purchased for educational, business, or sales
promotional use through our Special Markets Department.

HarperCollins Publishers Ltd
2 Bloor Street East, 20th Floor
Toronto, Ontario, Canada
M4W 1A8

www.harpercollins.ca

Library and Archives Canada Cataloguing in Publication information
is available upon request

ISBN: 978-1-44342-945-0

Printed and bound in Canada
DWF 9 8 7 6 5 4 3 2 1

Photographer: Edward Pond

For Barry Alper, our friend, our partner, and our equilibrium. We love you.

Many Thanks

To our publishers and editors for encouraging us and for being so excited about this cookbook from the very first day. Alison Maclean, Jennifer Smith, Lindsay Humphreys, Judy Phillips, and Ian Koo, thank you for your guidance, patience, and style.

To Edward Pond for your brilliant eye and lens. You captured the Fresh spirit, which is at the heart of everything we do.

To Barry Alper—there would be no Fresh without you. You are the unsung hero behind all of it.

To our strong head office team who keep it together for us all: Anita Brajkovic, Laura Duncan, and Nancy DeCaria. We are always at our best because of you.

To Gill—you are smart, funny, positive, perceptive, dedicated, and always calm. If we could clone you we could take over the world.

To Mogan, Vijay, and Josh—you are the backbone of Fresh. We genuinely appreciate everything you do. Thank you for the huge role you have played in our growth and success.

To our entire team of managers, both front and back of house, especially Meghan Pike, Gertrude Lung, Jessica Brousseau, Lynn Alexander, Megan Carriere, and Stephanie Weinz. Thanks for taking on the daily responsibilities and allowing us the freedom to do projects like this.

To Rasiah, Suganthan, Sri, Seelan, Ruben, and all of our dedicated dishwashers and cleaners. Thank you for keeping everything tidy and sparkling. Your hard work and positive attitudes are really appreciated.

To Henry Pak, for helping us to grow and thrive over the last 12 years. We wish you all the happiness in the world.

To Jeff Coussin, for doing everything that no one else can do. And for being hilarious in the process.

To Ilana at Sweets from the Earth, for providing us with the perfect complements to our menu. You are a groundbreaker and we're so happy to have you as part of our world.

To Rich Donsky at Mr. Produce and Roger at Fiormart—thank you for always going the extra mile for us. You're the best.

To Lisa Kiss of Lisa Kiss Design, for branding us with great colours and our fresh look.

To some special friends of Fresh: Phyllis Levine, Daniel Cytrynbaum, Kelly Rosin, David Dundas, Kim Harkness, Harvey Kotler, Bruce Haar, Rebecca Liu, Uday Kulkarni, Jeff Brown, Alanna Gerwitz, Frank Quattrociocchi, Lawrence Malek, Michael Chesney, Nigel Churcher, and Ralph Giannone.

To our loyal family of customers: those who have been coming to Fresh since the beginning, the thousands of others who have walked through the doors, and those of you across the world who have never set foot in a Fresh location but have experienced Fresh through our cookbooks. Your support and patronage has allowed us to grow, give back, and make our dreams come true.

To all the Fresh staff who appear in this book— you embody the fun, diverse, and colourful Fresh culture we are so proud of. You live in the pages of this book.

And to the entire family of front- and back-of-house staff at Fresh who keep us going, rain or shine. You fill the restaurants with your great style, warm service, hard work, and dedication. None of it would be possible without you.

RT + JH

RUTH'S THANKS

To my exuberant Tal family, pets included, for your unwavering love and encouragement. You are with me wherever I go.

Iris Tal and Robyn Levy, your courage astounds me. Your achievements are inspirational.

To my eclectic group of friends around the world who inspire me to live deep, think fast, and feel it all. Thank you for sheltering me, feeding me, squeezing me, and loving me during the writing of this cookbook.

Thank goodness for Kim Donnelly, Lisa Kelner, Bonnie Beecher, Alessandra De Oliveira, and Angelina Fraser. You kept me steady through the shifting tides of the past two years.

Renee Videla, Catherine Moeller, Sofia, Harley, and Croker: thank you for loving and caring for Maya in my absence as if she were your own.

A massive thank you is reserved for my Mexican and Costa Rican family of friends whose inspiration and influence is evident in this book: Diego Arce, Gaia Momo Arce, Ricardo Morales, Marion Peri, Moises Sayd, Franka Rosas Cavina, Quiahuatl A Kiaa, Paola Herrera, Leo Utskot, Alexander Utskot, Karla Moles, Adrian Arce, Lidia Fernandez, Christianne Guerrero Cajiga, Dave Paco, and Heidi Carter. You opened your homes, hearts, and kitchens to me. Mil besos.

Guadua Restaurant, Osa Mariposa, Dan's Deluxe Café, and La Luna Restaurant.

Entrepreneurs, movers, and mentors I love to know: Stewart Brown of Genuine Health; Kim Donnelly of CYKL; Cosimo Mammoliti of Terroni; Max Stefanelli of Terroni LA; Ralph Giannone, architect; Peter Primiani of the Communal Mule; Manolo Salinas, architect; Alina Felix; Notaria 14; Debra Berman of Berman & Co.; Silvana Kane of Pacifika; Beth Poulter of Kiska Designs; Claudio Aprile of Origin; Robbie Kane of Medina; Jeff Stober at the Drake Hotel; Allison Black and Nathan Morlando of Euclid 431 Pictures; Amba Stapleton of Nosara Yoga Institute; Gonca Gul of Ulla Sport; Nickodemus NYC; Ronnie Tal of Future Bright Insurance; Vicky Tal of Harvey Kalles; Nigel Churcher, worldwide art director; Carlo Rota; Nazneen Contractor; Michael Henry of INK; Michel Francoeur; and Claudia Gonzalez.

Finally, to the dogs: Maya, my 13-year-old Great Dane, and Frodo and Jonas, her handsome Labrador brothers in Puerto Escondido. Thank you for the licks!

JEN'S THANKS

The best part about having a book is getting to see the names of the people you care about in print. I used to fantasize when I was little about who I would thank if I got the chance. I guess if you're a budding singer or actor you would practice your acceptance speech in front of a mirror, but I always hoped to be published (a cookbook never occurred to me, but you never know what form your dreams will take), so composing my thank yous in my head was a frequent daydream. It's nice when your fantasies come true!

So, special thanks to:

My friends Chris MacLachlan, Kim Thompson, Melissa Curcumelli-Rodostamo, Katie Luedecke, Fiona Paterson, Jojo Steele, Gabrielle Shaw, Mary-Lynn Turk, Sarah Attwell, Erin Best Les-Pierre, and Jason Maguire, for adding joy to my life in so many ways.

My occasional sidekick, Maureen Maguire, for always going along with my plans; Michelle Vinassac, for keeping me balanced; and Reni Walker, Erin Stump, and Gianni Sabatino, for being great neighbours.

My favourite non-human friends, Sam, Tex, and MacGregor, for making me laugh every day.

My favourite children, Abby, Grace, and Jack Walker-Mitchell, Callum Smith and my goddaughter Ava Luedecke, for reminding me what it's like to be a kid.

And of course, my family: Barbara and Wayne Houston, Elizabeth Houston and Phyllis White, for everything.

Contents

We Are Fresh

Fresh is now a 150-person operation. This cookbook is written by the two of us, but the Fresh community goes way beyond just us. We have a huge team of staff, suppliers, and customers who make Fresh and the Fresh cookbooks a success.

Our managers, cooks, juicers, dishwashers, prep cooks, servers, hosts, cashiers, night cleaners, bookkeeper, and, of course, our partner, Barry, are the ones who keep the three locations running. Our staff members form their own little families within the whole: living together, and bringing their siblings, girlfriends, boyfriends, and best friends to work at Fresh. Staff work for us, go away to school, come back to work, go away for another job—or sometimes stay forever. We have some staff who have worked at Fresh for ten-plus years now, and that kind of commitment is very special in this industry.

The Fresh staff is diverse, but everyone is brought together by their commitment to hard work. By working side by side, they end up knowing each other's music, hearing each other's stories, taking up each other's causes, and always having each other's backs.

Fresh is constantly evolving, and it is our managers and staff who initiate ever better and more efficient ways of doing things. Fresh has seen a lot of changes and developments over the years. As we've grown, we've seen many faces come and go, and we are truly thankful to all of those who have contributed to our success.

The second branch of the Fresh family is our suppliers, who provide us daily with the raw ingredients that we turn into the Fresh menu. They work with us to bring the best the earth has to offer to the table, and we couldn't do it without their tireless efforts.

And finally, there's the biggest group of all, the Fresh customers, who, as well as being faithful to old standbys, explore new menu items with us, forgive us when we make a mistake, and share their passion for Fresh with their friends and families. They're loyal and honest, sharing their comments and feelings in order to let us know what we're doing right and to make us better. They speak our language, talking about Green Goddesses and Lung Lovers as though they are the most common things in the world. Some have been with us since the very beginning, some are just discovering Fresh, and many have had their first-ever vegetarian meal with us. To all of you, we are so grateful.

Together, we are Fresh: owners, staff, suppliers, customers, and you, the readers.

We hope that this latest collection of Fresh recipes inspires you and makes you feel a part of the Fresh community. In this book you will find what we think are our most inspired and exciting recipes yet. We are so happy to see vegan and vegetarian food being embraced by a wider population than ever before. And as its health and environmental benefits become validated and more widely accepted, it is even becoming a bit glamorous! Juicing and vegetarian cooking is getting further and further away from the old stereotypes as the years pass. As the meatless movement gains momentum worldwide, we are thrilled to be a part of it.

Thanks for being a part of Fresh, and please let us know how you enjoy these new recipes at feedback@ freshrestaurants.ca. We would love to hear from you.

Jennifer and Ruth

Fresh Food

My Path to Your Kitchen

Looking back, I realize I've always been slightly obsessed with food. I still have my childhood diaries in which I listed whatever we had for dinner that night and graded it. Shepherd's pie C+. Lasagna A–. And so on. If you read the diary I kept about my family's trip to the Maritimes when I was 10, you wouldn't learn very much about the sights, but you would know what we had for breakfast, lunch, and dinner every day! And I quote: "For breakfast, Liz [my sister] and I had a delicious pancake, it was huge—as big as a plate. It was like a crêpe and the edges were all nice and crispy." I still remember that pancake to this day. I'm not sure what most 10-year-olds write about in their diaries, but I doubt that there's a kid-style restaurant review on each page. The fact that I ended up cooking for a living shouldn't have come as such a surprise to me, but it did.

Although my very first job at the age of 15 was actually in a fast-food restaurant, I didn't cook in a restaurant again until I was 27, when I worked a shift in the kitchen at the pub where I was bartending and waitressing. From the minute I set foot in the kitchen, I knew that it was where I wanted to be. Within a year, I was at cooking school. Soon after, my friend Chris and I moved to Scotland.

Until then, I had mostly been cooking with meat, and vegetarianism wasn't even on my radar. In Scotland I got a job at a vegetarian restaurant and that was that. I became vegetarian almost right away. When I moved back to Toronto, I started working at Fresh (then called Juice for Life), and I knew that

this style of cooking was what I had been looking for. At cooking school, the goal was generally to work in fine dining, but I knew that casual food was much more up my alley because it was what I liked eating. I'm not sure why it took me until I was 28 to realize that I should be cooking for a living. But as soon as I did, I never looked back. When you find what you should be doing, you know it. And as soon as I started cooking vegetarian, I really knew that I had found my niche.

I think everyone's tastes change and evolve over the years, and I am no different. There is one side of me that is a total junk food lover, but the older I get, the less tolerance I have for it. Now when I have sugar or junk food, I need a nap half an hour later. The other side of me loves healthy food—beans, veggies, and everything we offer at Fresh. When I was on holiday in Jamaica a couple of years ago, I was very excited to find chickpeas at the salad bar. I never thought I would be so into chickpeas until I couldn't have them for a while! Now, more than ever, I am attracted to whole foods because I know they will make me feel good.

There are many reasons to be vegetarian, and I realized recently that I'm not vegetarian because I don't like the taste of meat, I'm vegetarian because I don't like everything that goes along with eating meat, like the cruelty, the harm to the environment, and all the other ethical implications. So I have made it my goal to prove to people who still eat meat that it is not the meat that makes the meal good. I hope that if people realize they can have a great taste experience without the meat, they will be more likely to go vegetarian at least part of the time, and that's a start.

I think the fact that I love mainstream flavours helps me to make vegetarian food that appeals to everyone. At Fresh, I try to make dishes that will appeal to both a junk food lover and a health food lover. I'm trying to take vegetarian food and make it crave-able. After all, I think as long as something tastes delicious, it doesn't matter if it's vegan or not. I proved this to myself a couple of years ago when I stayed with my dad while my mum went on holiday. My father, a quintessential meat-and-potatoes man, had recently suffered a stroke and wasn't able to cook for himself. I knew that this was going to be my biggest challenge yet: I was going to feed him a vegan diet and see how he liked it. Every time I put a plate in front of him, I waited for him to say something about missing the meat, but he never did. He loved the food! This proved to me that as long as a vegan meal tastes great, it can satisfy even the most diehard meat eaters.

In this book, I've tried to focus on showing you how to use dark green leafy vegetables as much as possible. It seems to me that whenever you read an article or see someone on TV talking about nutrition, they always say that you should get more dark green leafy vegetables into your diet, but I have a feeling that everyone just ignores it because they don't know what to do with greens. I did a quick little survey among my friends and it turns out I was right. I have tried to get leafy greens into as many recipes as possible so that you will be more comfortable using them and will get into the habit of always having them in the fridge.

This book is different from our previous ones in a couple of ways. This is the first time we have included non-vegan recipes in our cookbooks. On our menu, all the items are vegan, but our retail fridges stock salads and sandwiches that contain dairy, and we're sharing those recipes this time around. Second, some of the dishes in this book aren't available in the restaurants. They are my fantasy-menu items, the ones I would love to put on the menu if I could—if we had unlimited staff and time. Because we make almost everything ourselves, and there are only so many hours in the day and so many people we can fit in our kitchens, we can't offer every single thing that I dream up. Not that any of these recipes are difficult, but some of them just wouldn't fit into the restaurants' flow. Lots of the recipes in this book are from our menu, but it was very exciting for me to be able to create whatever I wanted to without thinking about whether or not we could actually execute it at Fresh. That's why I'm so glad to have this forum to share both the way I cook at home and how I cook for Fresh.

The most gratifying result of our previous cookbooks are the e-mails I get from people saying that they actually use and enjoy the recipes. When I'm creating them, I'm thinking about you at home; I try to anticipate any questions that might arise, so that making these recipes is easy and a pleasure for you. I hope I have succeeded and that you will really use this book. I like to imagine it lying open on your counter, splattered with food and dog-eared—that's my goal.

Jennifer

In the Kitchen

EQUIPMENT
To make the recipes in this book, you'll need just a few pieces of equipment.

Immersion blender
I use an immersion blender, also known as a hand blender or stick blender, all the time, especially for blending soups, because you can do it right in the pot, while they're still hot.

Julienne peeler or turning slicer
It's worth getting a julienne peeler for long, shredded veggies. If you try to grate vegetables on a box grater, you'll end up with little shreds that don't have much visual appeal. At Fresh, we use a turning slicer, also known as a spiralizer, which costs about $100. A good option for home use is a julienne peeler. Although it doesn't produce the super-long curly strands that a turning slicer does, a julienne peeler produces beautiful strands and costs only about $10.

Tongs
I don't understand how people cook without tongs—I can't live without them. Visit a restaurant supplier and choose the simplest metal tongs. Look for ones without a locking mechanism at the top and with flat points—not scoop-shaped—that meet up perfectly when squeezed together. They should cost only a few dollars.

Cheese plane
Using a cheese plane is the best way to get really thin slices of cheese—you'll never get them thin enough with a knife. It is also great for cutting zucchini really thin for, say, the Raw Lasagna (page 21).

INGREDIENTS
Sweeteners
Most sugar is refined using bone char, which is burned animal bones. However, organic sugar manufacturers don't use this method; that's why we always use organic sugar whenever sugar is called for. We use agave nectar and maple syrup where possible, but sometimes you just need the intense sweetness of cane sugar.

Spices
It's best to grind your spices just before using them. It really makes a difference to the taste. This goes for black pepper too. Don't ever use pre-ground pepper—it doesn't taste the same at all.

Garlic
Avoid using the chopped garlic that comes in a jar. I didn't think anyone actually used the stuff until a friend told me that her children didn't like her cooking. In trying to figure out why, we uncovered the fact that she uses garlic from a jar. It has a taste all its own, and it's not a good one.

Don't keep garlic in the fridge; keep it in the cupboard in a garlic keeper—a little pot with a lid and holes in it so the garlic can breathe.

Vegetable stock

You could make your own vegetable stock, but I know that it's much more realistic for most of us to buy it. My friend Chris called me one day when she was about to make a soup from *Fresh at Home*, one of our previous cookbooks, asking if she really had to make the vegetable stock for the recipe to work. I told her, of course not! You just need to know what to look for when buying stock. There is an ongoing debate about MSG. It is generally considered bad for us, so most manufacturers now label their stock powder with "no added MSG." But if you look at the ingredient list, you'll see disodium inosinate and disodium guanylate listed, which add up to—you guessed it—MSG. It's just broken down into two components. Others say that MSG is naturally occurring, so it is okay. I am not a scientist, but since there's so much conflicting information out there, I would rather not take a chance, so I make sure I buy one with no added MSG, no naturally occurring MSG, no MSG at all. Look for a stock that has only ingredients you recognize—nothing "hydrolyzed" and nothing with a chemical-sounding name.

Vegan cheese

Finally there is a vegan cheese that actually melts and tastes good. Vegans have been waiting a long time for Daiya to be invented! I like to use a mix of the cheddar and mozza flavours so that the finished dish isn't bright orange.

Cheese from milk

At Fresh, we use only rennet-free cheese. Rennet is an extract from the stomachs of certain animals, including cows or sheep. Some cheeses are labelled "rennet-free." If it's not, check the ingredient list to make sure there is no animal rennet listed. In North America, microbial and synthetic rennet are generally cheaper than animal rennet, so most cheese manufacturers use them instead. However, most European cheeses still use animal rennet.

Textured vegetable protein (TVP)

Textured vegetable protein (TVP) is made from the flour that's left after the oil has been extracted from soybeans. It is cooked under pressure, extruded, and dried. It comes in various sizes, from the small flakes that look like ground beef to the larger chunks and slices that resemble pieces of chicken when rehydrated. TVP takes on the flavour of whatever you cook it with and is great for vegetarians who miss the feeling of eating meat.

KITCHEN TIPS
To prep leeks

Cut off the roots and the tops. I've seen some recipes that ask you to cut off all of the green leaves, but I like to use the green parts too. Discard just the top third of the green part. Then cut the leeks in half lengthwise and slice. Put the sliced leeks in a large bowl and cover with water, swishing them around with your hands to separate the pieces and loosen any dirt. Let the leeks float for a few minutes so that the dirt sinks to the bottom of the bowl. Lift the leeks out of the water, transferring them to a colander and discarding the rinsing water. Clean the bowl, then return the leeks to the bowl, cover with water, and repeat the procedure until they're clean. Don't just pour the leeks from the bowl into the colander, because you'll be pouring the dirt right back over them. By lifting them out of the bowl, you'll leave the dirt behind.

Keeping vegetables and herbs fresh

Whenever I have veggies or herbs that are starting to go limp, I treat them like they are a bouquet of flowers: I cut off the stems and put them in a glass of water in the fridge. As they soak up the water, they will come back to life. This works for celery, broccoli, parsley—basically anything with a stem.

Appetizers

7 Layer Dip

This dip is great hot or cold. Serve it with tortilla chips, pita chips, or raw vegetables. One of my favourite veggies to use for dipping is Belgian endive. Just separate the leaves for perfect little scoops. To make pita chips, split a pita in half, cut each half into triangles, then toast in a 350°F oven on a baking sheet until crispy.

Serves 6 to 8 as an appetizer or as part of a buffet

1	batch Black Bean Mix (page 130)
1	batch Avocado Chipotle Sauce (page 103)
1 cup	chopped tomatoes
1	batch Cheesy Sauce (see below)
¼ cup	chopped red or green onion
1 cup	shredded iceberg lettuce
½ cup	chopped cilantro
½ cup	pickled jalapeño peppers (optional)

Cheesy Sauce

2 tsp	sunflower oil
½ cup	chopped onion
½ cup	chopped carrot
¼ cup	chopped celery
3	cloves garlic, sliced
¼ tsp	sea salt
1 cup	vegetable stock
½ cup	mozzarella-style Daiya vegan cheese
½ cup	cheddar-style Daiya vegan cheese
3 tbsp	water
2 tsp	lemon juice
1 tsp	Dijon mustard
¼ cup	sunflower oil
1 cup	silken tofu
½ tsp	sea salt
1 tsp	freshly ground black pepper
½ cup	chopped parsley

To make Cheesy Sauce

1. Heat 2 tsp sunflower oil in a frying pan over medium-low heat. Add onion, carrot, celery, garlic, and ¼ tsp sea salt. Cook, stirring often, until vegetables are softened but not browned.
2. Add stock, bring to a boil, reduce heat, and simmer until carrot is softened and most of the liquid has evaporated.
3. Add Daiya cheeses and stir until melted. Remove from heat and let cool (to speed this up, transfer the mixture to a bowl and put it in the fridge).
4. Once carrot mixture is cool, put the ingredients in a blender in the following order: water, lemon juice, mustard, ¼ cup sunflower oil, tofu, ½ tsp sea salt, pepper, carrot mixture, and parsley. Make sure the liquid is at the bottom of the blender by the blades.
5. Blend until smooth.

To assemble

1. Spread Black Bean Mix on the bottom of a large serving bowl if serving it cold, or of an oven-proof dish if serving it hot.
2. Top with Avocado Chipotle Sauce and spread to the edges.
3. Sprinkle tomatoes over top.
4. Spread Cheesy Sauce over and spread to edges.
5. If you are going to serve it cold, layer onion, lettuce, cilantro, and jalapeños on top, then refrigerate until ready to serve. If serving it hot, bake in a 350°F oven for 30 minutes or until heated through. Remove from oven and layer onion, lettuce, cilantro, and jalapeños on top.

Black Bean Tostada

Sprouted corn tortillas are available at health food stores and some supermarkets. If you can't find them, use regular corn tortillas.

At the restaurants we prep the carrot and yellow beets with a turning slicer or spiralizer. If you don't have one, use a julienne peeler or just cut them into long thin strips with a knife.

Serves 6

6	6-inch sprouted corn tortillas
3 cups	finely sliced napa cabbage
1	batch Avocado Chipotle Sauce (page 103)
1	batch Black Bean Mix (page 130)
6 tbsp	diced red onion
6 tbsp	diced red pepper
3 cups	spiralized or shredded carrot
1 ½ cups	sliced jicama (cut into small sticks)
1 ½ cups	spiralized or shredded yellow beets
	chopped cilantro

1. Heat tortillas in a toaster, grill, frying pan, or oven.

2. On each of 6 plates, spread ½ cup napa cabbage. This will hold the tortilla in place on the plate.

3. Spread each tortilla with ¼ cup Avocado Chipotle Sauce and place on top of cabbage, sauce-side up.

4. Divide Black Bean Mix, red onion, red pepper, carrot, jicama, and beets among tortillas. Top with as much cilantro as you like.

Dukkah

This easy appetizer will really make your taste buds sing. Serve it with toasted pita or bread and olive oil. Simply dip the bread in the oil and then in the dukkah.

Toasting the seeds isn't optional in this recipe; it is an essential step to get the right flavour. Traditionally, the nuts are roasted too, but we like to leave those raw.

Serves 4 to 6

1 tbsp	coriander seeds
1 tbsp	cumin seeds
1 tbsp	fennel seeds
¼ cup	finely chopped hazelnuts
¼ cup	finely chopped pistachios
2 tbsp	sesame seeds
2 tbsp	flaxseed meal
1 tsp	sea salt
1 tsp	freshly ground black pepper

1. Heat coriander, cumin, and fennel seeds in a small frying pan over medium-high heat, shaking or stirring often.
2. When spices are very fragrant and starting to darken, remove from heat and grind in a spice grinder.
3. Put spices and remaining ingredients in a small bowl and stir to mix.

Middle Eastern Platter

One of our most popular appetizers at Fresh, this is a tasty combination of herbed falafel balls, flax hummus, quinoa tabouleh, toasted pita, and three delicious sauces. It's great for a buffet or party. You could also just serve the falafel balls in a pita with the three sauces. Just stuff a pita with fresh veggies, lettuce, and a few falafel balls, drizzle with tahini, and serve the amba and zhug on the side. The quinoa tabouleh is great on its own as well, perhaps topped with Grilled Tofu Steaks (page 131), for a light lunch.

Serves 6 to 8 people

6 to 8	flaxseed pitas
1	batch Zhug (page 111)
1	batch Amba (page 102)
1	batch Tahini Sauce (page 111)

Herb Falafel Balls

Makes 30 falafel balls

2	cloves garlic
½ cup	chopped cilantro
½ cup	chopped fresh mint
½ cup	chopped parsley
1	can (19 oz/540 ml) chickpeas, drained and rinsed
½ cup	bread crumbs
½ cup	spelt flour
⅓ cup	finely diced onion
4 tbsp	tahini
1 tsp	baking powder
1 tsp	sea salt
1 tsp	ground coriander
¼ to ½ cup	sunflower oil, for cooking

1. Mince garlic in a food processor. Add cilantro, mint, and parsley and pulse until finely chopped. Transfer to a large bowl.

2. Put chickpeas in food processor and pulse to chop finely, but don't purée.

3. Add chickpeas and remaining ingredients, except oil, to bowl. Mix everything together thoroughly with your hands.

4. Form into small balls (1 tbsp each) and press together between your palms to pack together and flatten slightly. Set aside in the fridge to cook later, or cook right away, either in a frying pan or the oven (frying makes them crispier and more like traditional falafel).

5. To cook in the oven, preheat oven to 350°F. Place falafel balls on a baking sheet and brush tops lightly with sunflower oil. Bake for 20 minutes, turning over and brushing with a bit more oil halfway through.

6. Or, heat oil in a frying pan and cook over medium-high heat, flipping to brown on both sides, until heated through and crispy.

Quinoa Tabouleh

1 cup	quinoa
1 ½ cups	vegetable stock
½ cup	chopped English cucumber
½ cup	chopped parsley
¼ cup	shelled edamame
¼ cup	chopped raw, unsalted cashews
¼ cup	chopped tomato
2 tbsp	finely chopped red onion

1. Rinse quinoa a few times until water runs clear. Put quinoa and stock in a rice cooker or pot and cook until all stock is absorbed. Spread out onto a baking sheet to cool.
2. Meanwhile, make the dressing (see below).
3. Once quinoa is cool, transfer to a large bowl. Add remaining ingredients and dressing, tossing well to mix.

Dressing

1	clove garlic, minced
2 tbsp	lemon juice
1 tbsp	rice vinegar
1 ½ tsp	lemon zest
1 ½ tsp	Dijon mustard
1 ½ tsp	agave nectar
¼ tsp	sea salt
¼ tsp	freshly ground black pepper
3 tbsp	sunflower oil
2 tbsp	olive oil

1. Put all ingredients except oils in a blender or food processor and blend.
2. Gradually add oil, in drops at first and then in a small stream. Don't pour it in too fast or the dressing won't emulsify.
3. Or, put the ingredients in a bowl and whisk in the oil by hand.

Flax Hummus

2	cloves garlic
1	can (19 oz/540 ml) chickpeas, drained and rinsed
½ to ¾ cup	water
2 tbsp	olive oil
2 tbsp	lemon juice
2 tbsp	flaxseed meal
1 tbsp	tahini
1 tsp	sea salt
⅛ tsp	ground cumin
¼ tsp	ground coriander

1. Mince garlic in a food processor.
2. Add remaining ingredients and process until smooth. Start with just ½ cup water, and add the remaining ¼ cup if needed.

To assemble platter
1. Arrange the falafel balls, quinoa tabouleh, and flax hummus on a platter, with toasted pita triangles and bowls of the three sauces on the side.

Quinoa Onion Rings

These onion rings have taken the Fresh world by storm. I'm not going to lie to you, they are very fiddly to make. Just be glad you don't have to make hundreds of them at a time like we do! You will find puffed quinoa in the cereal section of health food stores. If you can't find it, use puffed millet instead.

Makes 20 to 24 large onion rings

1	Spanish onion, cut into 20 to 24 thick rings (save smaller end rings for another use)
1 cup	flour of your choice (e.g., all-purpose, spelt, gluten-free)
4 cups	canola oil, for frying

Batter

½ cup	flour of your choice (e.g., all-purpose, spelt, gluten-free)
¼ tsp	sea salt
¼ tsp	baking powder
¼ tsp	curry powder (optional)
¼ cup	unsweetened, unflavoured soy milk
¼ cup	water

Quinoa Coating

1 ½ cups	puffed quinoa
1 ½ cups	bread crumbs
1 tsp	sea salt
1 tsp	garlic powder

1. For batter, combine ½ cup flour, sea salt, baking powder, and curry powder in a shallow bowl. Pour in soy milk and water, stirring to mix.
2. For the quinoa coating, combine quinoa, bread crumbs, sea salt, and garlic powder in a shallow bowl.
3. In a plastic bag, toss the onion rings with 1 cup flour.
4. Dip 1 or 2 onion rings in the batter, coating all surfaces.
5. Place the rings in the quinoa coating, coating all surfaces. You may have to press the coating on.
6. Repeat until all the rings are coated. Place the coated rings on a baking sheet, cover with plastic wrap, and refrigerate for at least 30 minutes and up to 8 hours or overnight to firm up.
7. Heat oil in a large saucepan to 350°F. A good way to tell if your oil is hot enough is to stick a wooden chopstick or the end of a wooden spoon into the oil. If bubbles form all over it, your oil is hot enough.
8. Drop onion rings into the oil and cook a few at a time until browned and crispy. Don't over-crowd your pan. Drain on paper towel and serve.

Raw Asparagus Noodles

If you like cooked asparagus, chances are you'll love it raw as well. This is a very simple dish that really highlights the taste of the asparagus and all the elements of the Protein Boost.

Serves 2 as an appetizer

6 to 10	spears asparagus
¼ cup	Protein Boost (page 133)
2 tsp	olive or flax oil
½ tsp	lemon juice
¼ tsp	sea salt

1. Holding an asparagus spear by its root end, use a very sharp peeler to shave it into tendrils by peeling down its length, rotating the spear every so often. You will be left with some bits that can't be shaved; cut these into thin pieces with a knife. Discard the woody end. Repeat with remaining spears. You should end up with about 2 cups shaved asparagus.
2. Toss asparagus and remaining ingredients together in a bowl, then pile onto 2 plates.

Raw Lasagna

This dish is a great introduction to the world of raw food. Choose a zucchini that is about 8 inches long, or the same length as your pan, so that each slice fits in it perfectly. You could also use jicama for the "pasta"—just cut it as thin as possible, preferably using a mandolin. It will stay crunchy, whereas zucchini will be soft. You'll be making four mixes in the food processor, but you don't need to wash it between mixtures—it's all going in the same place. Prepare the walnut layer first, then the cauliflower, pesto, and tomato sauce (soak the sun-dried tomatoes for the tomato sauce while you're preparing the other mixes). The pesto recipe makes more than you'll need for the lasagna, so either make a quarter of the recipe or make it all and use the leftovers in other dishes. If you can't find micro arugula, use any kind of sprouts you like, or finely shred regular arugula.

Serves 6

1	large zucchini
3 cups	micro arugula, for garnish

Walnut Mixture

1 cup	chopped walnuts
2 tsp	lemon juice
1 tsp	coconut oil
¼ tsp	sea salt

Cauliflower Mixture

2 cups	chopped cauliflower
3 tbsp	olive oil
½ tsp	sea salt

Pesto

6 tsp	Pesto (see page 109)

Tomato Sauce

½ cup	sun-dried tomatoes, soaked in water for 1 hour
1 cup	chopped tomatoes
2 tbsp	olive oil
1 tbsp	chopped green onion
1 ½ tsp	agave nectar
½ tsp	sea salt
½ tsp	lemon juice
⅛ tsp	crushed dried chilies or 1 fresh red Thai chili

To make mixtures

1. For walnut mixture, process ingredients together in food processor until finely minced but not puréed.
2. For cauliflower mixture, pulse ingredients for a few seconds until finely minced but not puréed. Scrape down cauliflower with a spatula if it spreads up the sides of the processor.
3. For pesto, prepare according to recipe directions.
4. For tomato sauce, drain sun-dried tomatoes, then pulse in a food processor, scraping down sides a few times, until finely chopped. Add remaining ingredients and process until combined.

To assemble

1. Line an 8-inch square pan with plastic wrap, leaving overlap on all edges.
2. Cut zucchini into thin slices with a mandolin, cheese plane, peeler, or knife.
3. Lay zucchini in the pan in a single layer, slightly overlapping slices.
4. Spread walnut mix over zucchini.
5. Top with another layer of zucchini. Spread tomato sauce over top, and then cauliflower mix.
6. Top with another layer of zucchini.
7. Put a cutting board on top of pan, turn both upside-down, and let lasagna fall out onto the board. Remove plastic wrap.
8. Using a sharp serrated knife, cut into 6 portions. Transfer each portion to a serving plate and garnish with 1 tsp pesto and ½ cup arugula.

Sweet Potato Fries

I didn't include the recipe for our sweet potato fries in our previous cookbooks, but enough people have asked how to make them that I thought it was time—so here you go.

To get the oil to the right temperature for blanching, use a thermometer if you have one, but if you don't, test it by dropping one fry into the hot oil. If, after a few minutes, it is softened but not browned, your oil is at the perfect temperature. If the fry is browned but not soft, reduce the heat a bit. When blanching, there will be a constant gentle bubbling rising from the fries if the oil is at the right temperature. If there are no bubbles, increase the heat, and if there are crazy, out-of-control bubbles, turn it down. For the final cooking, the oil needs to be even hotter, but not so hot that the fries over-brown.

At Fresh, we toss our fries with Mixed Herbs (page 131), but if you have any fresh herbs on hand, especially thyme, oregano, or rosemary, chop those up very finely and toss the fries in them, along with the sea salt.

We don't peel our sweet potatoes, but if you prefer yours peeled, feel free.

Serves 4 to 6

6 cups	fry-cut sweet potatoes (cut into sticks) or 1 bag (24 oz/680 g) precut sweet potatoes
4 cups	canola oil
	sea salt
	Mixed Herbs (page 131)

1. Heat oil in a large pot over medium-low heat to about 275°F. Blanch sweet potatoes in the oil by letting them cook for 5 to 6 minutes, until they are bendy but not coloured. You may have to do this in batches, depending on how big the pot is.
2. Remove fries from oil using a slotted spoon, put onto baking sheet, and set aside to cool on the counter or in the fridge for at least 1 hour and up to 8 hours or overnight.
3. Let oil cool, and set aside to use later.
4. When ready to serve the fries, heat the oil over high heat to about 375°F.
5. Add blanched fries and cook for a few minutes, until browned to your liking.
6. Remove fries from oil and toss in a large bowl with sea salt and Mixed Herbs.

Soup

Beans, Greens, and Stars

I love cute little pasta stars. They really appeal to the kid in me. If you can't find stars, use alphabets, orzo, baby shells, or any other little shaped pasta you like. If you're reheating leftovers of this soup, you'll need to add more stock because it thickens up as it sits.

Serves 4 to 6

2 tbsp	olive oil
1 cup	chopped carrot
1 cup	diced onion
3	cloves garlic, minced
½ tsp	dried oregano
5 cups	vegetable stock
1 cup	pasta stars or any other tiny pasta or thin noodle
1	can (19 oz/540 ml) white kidney beans, drained and rinsed
4 cups	finely chopped mixed leafy greens (e.g., kale, bok choy, Swiss chard)
	sea salt
	freshly ground black pepper

1. Heat oil in a large pot over medium-high heat. Add carrot, onion, and garlic. Cook until softened, stirring often.
2. Stir in oregano.
3. Add stock, pasta, and beans. Cook, stirring often so pasta doesn't stick to bottom of pot, until pasta is tender but firm.
4. Stir in mixed greens, bring soup back to a boil, reduce heat, and simmer for a few minutes, until greens are tender.
5. Season with salt and pepper to taste.
6. If you like a clear broth, leave the soup as is. If you prefer a creamier texture, transfer 3 cups of the soup to a separate container, purée with an immersion blender, then return it to the pot and bring back to a boil before serving.

The Best Carrot Soup

Billy Steele, a Glasgow chef who is married to my friend Jojo, made this soup during one of my visits. I hesitated to ask him what was in it because it was so delicious, I thought maybe it was a secret, complicated recipe he wouldn't want to share. But it turns out to be the simplest recipe ever, and he was happy to share it with me.

If you are vegan, skip the parmesan cheese, or replace it with a few flakes of nutritional yeast or a sprinkling of Vegan Parmesan Coating (page 52). If you want to elevate this soup a little to serve it at a dinner party, garnish it with truffle oil and pine nuts. This soup is at its best and creamiest when it's served right away.

Serves 6

4 tbsp	olive oil, plus extra for garnishing
4 cups	diced onions
8 cups	chopped carrots
10 cups	vegetable stock
½ tsp	sea salt
	freshly grated parmesan cheese

1. Heat oil in a large pot over medium heat.
2. Add onions and cook a few minutes until softened.
3. Add carrots and stock, bring to a boil, reduce heat, and then simmer until carrots are softened.
4. Add salt and then purée mixture with an immersion blender. Taste and add more salt if needed.
5. Serve garnished with a drizzle of olive oil and freshly grated parmesan cheese.

Creamy Celery and Cashew Purée

Our partner, Barry Alper, is always wishing we had more celery on our menu, so I made this soup for him, even though I'm not a huge celery fan. Turns out he was really only interested in raw celery! Anyway, I'm glad I made this soup because it has made me love celery. The cashews and rice milk give it an amazing creaminess.

Serves 6

2 tbsp	Earth Balance
4 tsp	olive oil
12 cups	chopped celery
4	cloves garlic, minced
1 cup	raw cashew pieces
4 cups	vegetable stock
2 cups	unsweetened, unflavoured rice milk
1 tsp	sea salt
	freshly ground black pepper

1. Heat Earth Balance and olive oil in a large pot over medium heat.
2. Add celery and garlic. Cook until the garlic is fragrant.
3. Add the cashews, stock, rice milk, and sea salt. Bring to a boil, reduce heat, and simmer until celery is softened.
4. Purée with an immersion blender.
5. Add pepper to taste and more salt if needed.

Butternut Squash with Sage and Roasted Garlic Soup

I know five heads of garlic seems like a lot for one pot of soup, but because it's roasted, the flavour is mellow and nutty and not overpowering at all. It's a perfect complement to the squash. If you like, buy peeled and chopped squash, available in many supermarkets.

The nuts and seeds in the Protein Boost also really complement this soup and make every mouthful slightly different, so don't skip this garnish.

Serves 6

5	heads garlic
1 ¼ tsp + 2 tbsp	canola oil
	sea salt
1	butternut squash (about 6 cups chopped)
4 cups	chopped onions
2	stalks celery, chopped
¼ tsp	nutmeg
6	fresh sage leaves, chopped, or ½ tsp dried
6 to 8 cups	vegetable stock
4 cups	peeled and chopped potato
	freshly ground black pepper
6 tbsp	Protein Boost (page 133)

1. Preheat oven to 350°F.
2. Remove loose skin from garlic and cut tops off so that the top of each clove is exposed. Place on a baking sheet, drizzle each head with ¼ tsp canola oil and sprinkle with a pinch of salt.
3. Roast in oven for about 30 minutes or until softened. Meanwhile prepare squash (see Step 4). Once soft, remove garlic from oven and let cool.
4. Using a strong, sharp knife, cut off both ends of the squash, then cut it in half where it starts to flare out. Peel each half with the knife. Cut the bulb-shaped section in half and use a spoon to scoop out the seeds. Chop the squash into large chunks.
5. Heat 2 tbsp canola oil in a large pot over medium-high heat. Add onions and celery, and cook until softened.
6. Stir in nutmeg and cook for a few seconds. Add squash, sage, 6 cups of the stock, and potato. Bring to a boil, reduce heat, and simmer until vegetables are softened, about 20 minutes.
7. While the soup is cooking, squeeze all the roasted garlic out of the skins and set aside. Once the vegetables in the soup are soft, add the roasted garlic.
8. Purée soup with an immersion blender and add salt and pepper to taste. If the soup is too thick, add the remaining stock and bring back to a boil.
9. Garnish each bowl with 1 tbsp Protein Boost.

Broccoli and Cauliflower Purée

There's nothing like a great broccoli soup, and this one is especially good because of the addition of leeks and cauliflower. The Dijon adds a subtle tangy note. You can use the stems of the broccoli when making this soup—simply cut off the ends and the peel and chop the tender centre.

Serves 6

4 tbsp	canola oil
4 cups	sliced leeks
6	cloves garlic, minced
3 cups	chopped broccoli
3 cups	chopped cauliflower
1 ½ cups	peeled and diced potato
5 cups	vegetable stock
2 tsp	Dijon mustard
1 cup	unsweetened, unflavoured rice milk
	sea salt
	freshly ground black pepper

1. Heat oil in a large pot over medium heat.
2. Add leeks and garlic. Cook until softened.
3. Add broccoli, cauliflower, potato, stock, and mustard. Cook until vegetables are softened.
4. Add rice milk and bring mixture to a boil.
5. Purée with an immersion blender.
6. Add salt and pepper to taste.

Creamy Corn Chowder with Swiss Chard

This soup really highlights the sweetness of the corn. It is great without the Swiss chard too, if you don't have that on hand.

Serves 4 to 6

2 tbsp	canola oil
2	onions, chopped
2	stalks celery, chopped
2	carrots, peeled and chopped
2 cups	sliced leeks
6	cloves garlic, minced
pinch	nutmeg
2	potatoes, peeled and diced
2 cups	vegetable stock
1 tsp	sea salt
1 tsp	freshly ground black pepper
2 cups	unsweetened, unflavoured rice milk
2 cups	frozen corn kernels, rinsed
1 cup	chopped Swiss chard

1. Heat oil in a large pot over medium-high heat.
2. Add onions, celery, carrots, leeks, and garlic. Cook, stirring occasionally, until softened.
3. Stir in the nutmeg.
4. Add potatoes, stock, sea salt, and pepper. Bring to a boil, reduce heat, and simmer until potatoes are softened.
5. With an immersion blender, purée soup until about half of it is puréed and the rest is still chunky.
6. Add rice milk, corn, and Swiss chard. Bring soup back to a boil and let cook for 1 or 2 minutes, until the corn is heated through and the chard is softened.

Creamy Celery Root Purée

If you've never tried celeriac (aka celery root), you should. It looks kind of ugly, but if you can get past that, it's totally worth it. People sometimes describe it as tasting like a cross between celery and potato, and that's a pretty good description, but it's tastier than that. This soup is simple, to allow the subtleties of the celeriac to come through. To peel one of these little lovelies, use a paring knife to cut off the gnarly outer layer until you are left with the beautiful white flesh.

Serves 4 to 6

3 tbsp	canola oil
½ cup	white wine
1 ½ cups	chopped celery
1 ½ cups	chopped onion
3 cups	peeled and chopped celeriac (about 2 large celeriacs)
1 ½ cups	peeled and chopped potato
5 cups	vegetable stock
½ tsp	sea salt

1. Heat oil in a large pot over medium-high heat.
2. Add celery and onion and cook until softened, stirring often.
3. Add wine and let cook about 1 minute, until reduced by half.
4. Add remaining ingredients. Bring to a boil, reduce heat, and simmer until celeriac is softened.
5. Purée with an immersion blender.
6. Add more salt if needed.

Creamy Broccoli with Vegan Cheddar Soup

Get ready for a blast from the past if you haven't had broccoli and cheese soup for a while—especially if you're vegan. If you prefer, you can use only one type of Daiya vegan cheese, but if you use the orange one, the soup will have a bit of a Kraft Dinner–like colour to it. Kids will probably love that though, come to think of it! You can use the stems of the broccoli—just cut off the ends and the peel and use the tender centre. We purée three-quarters of the soup and leave the rest chunky, but you can decide those ratios for yourself. If you like a really smooth soup, purée it all; if you like more chunks, purée only a quarter of it.

Serves 6

2 tsp	canola oil
2 tsp	Earth Balance
1 cup	chopped onion
¾ cup	chopped carrot
1 tbsp	brown rice flour
2 cups	unsweetened, unflavoured rice or soy milk
1 cup	cheddar-style Daiya vegan cheese
1 cup	mozzarella-style Daiya vegan cheese
4 cups	vegetable stock
6 cups	chopped broccoli
	sea salt (optional)

1. Heat oil and Earth Balance in a large pot over medium heat.
2. Add onion and carrot and cook until softened, stirring often.
3. Add flour and cook for 1 or 2 minutes, stirring constantly.
4. Gradually add rice milk, in small amounts (about ¼ cup) at first, stirring to fully incorporate milk in between additions to prevent lumps.
5. Add vegan cheese and stir until melted.
6. Add stock, gradually at first, stirring to prevent lumps. Once soup is thin, pour remaining stock in all at once.
7. Add broccoli. Bring mixture to a boil, reduce heat, and simmer until broccoli is tender, about 5 minutes.
8. Remove one-quarter of the soup to a separate container and purée the rest with an immersion blender. Return non-puréed soup to the pot and stir to mix.
9. Add salt if needed and serve.

Creole Red Bean Soup

Allspice adds a spicy depth to this rich red soup. It is the perfect lunch for a cold, snowy day, with a big chunk of multigrain bread to dip in it.

Serves 4 to 6

1 tbsp	canola oil
1 cup	chopped onion
½ cup	chopped carrot
½ cup	chopped celery
1	clove garlic, minced
¾ tsp	allspice
¾ tsp	dried thyme or 1 ½ tsp fresh
¼ tsp	cayenne pepper
1	green pepper, chopped
2 cups	canned tomatoes
1	can (19 oz/540 ml) red kidney beans, drained and rinsed
4 cups	vegetable stock
½ tsp	Dijon mustard
1 tsp	molasses

1. Heat oil in a large pot over medium heat.
2. Add onion, carrot, celery, and garlic. Cook until softened.
3. Stir in allspice, thyme, and cayenne. Cook for 1 or 2 minutes.
4. Stir in green pepper and cook until softened.
5. Add tomatoes, beans, and stock. Bring to a boil, then reduce heat and let simmer for at least 10 and up to 30 minutes.
6. In a small bowl, mix the mustard and molasses with 1 or 2 tbsp of the broth from the soup. Add to the soup and stir well.

Curry Laksa

This broth is my version of a laksa, a classic Malaysian soup. I first had it on a holiday in Australia, where you can find it everywhere. I've never understood why it isn't as popular in Canada. Although laksa traditionally contains fish, this vegan version captures the essence of the original.

Tamarind paste has a sweet-and-sour taste that adds a depth of flavour. It comes mainly in two forms: a square block of concentrate with seeds and a seedless paste in a tub. This recipe calls for the concentrate. If you have seedless tamarind paste, mix it directly into the spice paste, without reconstituting it. If you can't find tamarind, substitute a teaspoon of lemon juice and a pinch of sugar.

The rice noodles that we use come in a 1 lb (454 g) package. The whole package will make 9 cups of noodles when cooked, so either cook just two-thirds of the noodles or cook all of them and use the leftovers for another dish. If you do have leftover noodles, rinse them a couple of times before refrigerating so they don't stick together in one big lump.

If you have any laksa broth left over, use it to make Laksa Rice (page 89).

Serves 6

2 cups	dried TVP chunks
1 tbsp	tamarind paste
1 tbsp	curry powder
1 tbsp	ground coriander (preferably freshly toasted and ground)
4 tsp	sambal oelek
1 ½ tsp	turmeric
½ tsp	sea salt
½ tsp	freshly ground black pepper
2 tbsp	canola oil
2 cups	chopped onion
2 tbsp	peeled and grated or minced ginger
1 tbsp	minced garlic
7 cups	vegetable stock
1	can (14 oz/400 ml) coconut milk

Garnishes

3 cups	baby spinach
6 cups	cooked rice noodles, prepared according to package directions
	fresh basil and cilantro leaves

1. Bring about 4 to 6 cups water to a boil in a large pot. Turn off heat and add TVP. Stir, then let sit for 15 to 20 minutes to rehydrate. Drain.

2. For broth, bring ¼ cup water to a boil in a small pot. Add the tamarind paste, break it apart a bit with a spoon, and let soak for a few minutes.

3. Meanwhile, in a small bowl, mix together curry powder, coriander, sambal oelek, turmeric, sea salt, and pepper. Set aside.

4. Heat oil in a large pot over medium-high heat. Add onion, ginger, and garlic and stir.

5. Put a fine mesh strainer over the bowl containing the spice mixture and pour the tamarind and water through the strainer into the bowl. Using a spoon, push the pulp through the strainer. Discard whatever solids are left in the strainer (but be sure to add any paste that collects on the underside of the strainer to the spices). Stir the tamarind into the spice mixture to combine.

6. Once the onions are softened, add the spices and cook for 1 or 2 minutes.

7. Add 1 cup of the stock and purée mixture with an immersion blender. Be careful not to splatter the broth, as turmeric can stain.
8. Add remaining stock, coconut milk, and TVP. Bring broth to a boil, reduce heat, and let simmer for 10 to 15 minutes, stirring occasionally.
9. To serve, place ½ cup spinach and 1 cup cooked rice noodles in the bottom of each of 6 large soup bowls. Pour 1 ¼ to 1 ½ cups of hot broth and TVP over top. Sprinkle with a few cilantro and basil leaves.

Winter Vegetable Chowder

The mix of vegetables called for in this recipe is what we use at Fresh, but you could easily substitute your favourites or whatever you have on hand. Celeriac, Brussels sprouts, or squash would all work well in this recipe. You can purée this soup a little or a lot, depending on how chunky you like your soups. The Fibre Boost (page 133) is a great addition to this hearty soup, adding crunch and different flavours to every bite.

Serves 4 to 6

2 tbsp	canola oil
2 cups	chopped onion
2 cups	sliced leeks
1 cup	chopped celery
⅓ cup	peeled and chopped parsnip
1 cup	peeled and chopped sweet potato
1 cup	peeled and chopped white potato
1 cup	chopped carrot
1 ½ cups	chopped cauliflower
½ tsp	dried thyme or 1 tsp fresh
5 cups	vegetable stock
½ tsp	sea salt
4 to 6 tbsp	Fibre Boost (page 133)

1. Heat oil in a large pot over medium heat.
2. Add onion, leeks, and celery and cook until softened.
3. Add remaining ingredients (except the Fibre Boost), bring to a boil, reduce heat, and simmer until vegetables are tender.
4. With an immersion blender, purée soup to your liking.
5. Add more salt if needed.
6. Pour into bowls and garnish with Fibre Boost.

Leek, Sweet Potato, and Kale Soup

This soup is on the thinner, lighter side, so if you would like a thicker, heartier texture, add a bit less stock. For instructions on how to clean leeks, see page 9.

Serves 4 to 6

2 tbsp	canola oil
4 cups	chopped leeks
4 cups	peeled and chopped sweet potato
8 cups	vegetable stock
2 tsp	fresh thyme
	sea salt
1 cup	chopped kale

1. Heat oil in a large pot over medium heat.
2. Add leeks. Sauté until softened.
3. Add sweet potato, stock, and thyme, bring to a boil, then reduce heat and simmer until sweet potato is softened. Remove half of soup to a separate container and purée with an immersion blender, then return to pot, stirring to combine.
4. Add salt to taste.
5. Add kale, bring soup back to a boil, reduce heat, and cook for a few minutes until kale is tender.

Parsnip, Apple, and Roasted Chestnut Purée

This soup tastes like Christmas dinner in a bowl. If you want to increase the Christmas factor even more, add a pinch of sage. You can buy the chestnuts roasted and peeled in 3.5 oz (100 g) bags at most supermarkets in the winter months. If you like, garnish this soup with a sprinkling of Omega Shake (page 133).

Serves 4 to 6

2 tbsp	canola oil
1 ½ cups	sliced leeks
1 cup	chopped onion
2 cups	peeled and chopped potato
1 ¼ cups	peeled and chopped parsnips
4 cups	vegetable stock
1	pkg (3.5 oz/100 g) roasted, peeled chestnuts
1 cup	peeled and chopped apple
½ cup	unsweetened, unflavoured rice milk
	sea salt
	freshly ground black pepper

1. Heat oil in a large pot over medium-high heat.
2. Add leeks and onion. Cook until softened, stirring often.
3. Add potato, parsnips, stock, chestnuts, and apple. Bring to a boil, reduce heat, and simmer until vegetables are softened, about 20 to 30 minutes.
4. Add rice milk and purée with an immersion blender. Bring mixture to a boil.
5. Season with salt and pepper to taste.

Fresh Pho

This soup has a long history, but not a vegan one. To emulate the rich stock, which is traditionally beef based, I've used lots of onions, garlic, and mushrooms, as well as the classic spices: star anise, cinnamon, and cloves. You can add any kind of vegetables that you like to this soup. The baby spinach is so delicate that it doesn't need to be pre-cooked, but if using broccoli or greens, boil them in the broth until tender before pouring the soup over the noodles. The traditional garnishes are hoisin sauce, Sriracha, and lime wedges. If you have these on hand, use them, though the soup is also great without.

Do you know the difference between regular hoisin sauce and vegetarian hoisin sauce? Neither contain animal products, but the vegetarian version doesn't have any onions or garlic—Buddhists and Hare Krishnas don't eat either of these because they feel that they have the quality of passion, which can interrupt spiritual balance.

The rice noodles that we use come in a 1 lb (454 g) package. The whole package will make 9 cups of noodles when cooked, so either cook just two-thirds of the noodles or cook all of them and use the leftovers for another dish. If you do have leftover noodles, rinse them a couple of times before refrigerating so they don't stick together in one big lump.

Serves 6

Marinated Soy Slices

2 cups	dried TVP slices
¾ cup	organic sugar
½ cup	soy sauce
½ cup	water
2 tbsp	sunflower oil
1 tbsp	sesame oil
1	clove garlic, minced
1 tsp	grated ginger

Broth

2 tbsp	canola oil
2	onions, halved and then quartered
½ cup	coarsely chopped garlic
3 cups	sliced mushroom
¼ tsp	Chinese five-spice powder
⅔ cup	sliced ginger
8	whole cloves
6	star anise
1	cinnamon stick
8 cups	vegetable stock

Garnishes

3 cups	baby spinach
6 cups	cooked rice noodles, prepared according to package directions
1 ½ cups	bean sprouts
¾ cup	chopped cilantro
24	fresh basil leaves
6 tbsp	pumpkin seeds
2 tbsp	chopped green onions

1. For marinated soy slices, bring 4 to 6 cups water to a boil in a large pot. Turn off heat and add TVP. Stir, then let sit for 15 to 20 minutes to rehydrate. Drain.
2. Put all marinade ingredients in a large bowl and stir to dissolve sugar.
3. Add rehydrated TVP and toss with marinade. Marinate for at least 1 hour in the fridge
4. For broth, heat oil in a large pot over high heat. Add onions, garlic, and mushrooms. Cook until well browned, stirring often.
5. Stir in Chinese five-spice powder and cook for a few seconds.
6. Add ginger, cloves, star anise, cinnamon, and stock. Bring to a boil, reduce heat, and simmer, uncovered, for 1 hour.
7. Strain through a fine-mesh strainer and discard solids.
8. Place broth and TVP in a pot over high heat and bring to a boil.
9. To serve, put ½ cup baby spinach and 1 cup cooked rice noodles in the bottom of each of 6 large soup bowls. Pour hot stock and TVP over top.
10. Distribute bean sprouts, cilantro, basil, pumpkin seeds, and green onions among the bowls.
11. Serve with hoisin sauce, Sriracha hot sauce, and wedges of lime.

White Bean and Butternut Squash Chili with Smoked Paprika

When I was little, my mum often made chili, always accompanied by what I thought was "special toast." I'm not sure what I thought was so special about it, but it tasted so good with the chili that I didn't think it could possibly be just regular toast. Once I was old enough to start helping prepare the meals, my mum asked me to make the toast to go with the chili. "But I don't know how to make the special toast!" I said. She laughed, because it turns out it was just regular toast with butter. It wasn't even special bread, just plain old sliced whole wheat. Anyway, try some of your own special toast with this delicious hearty and smoky chili.

Serves 6

3 tbsp	canola oil
1 ½ cups	chopped onion
3	cloves garlic, minced
4 cups	quartered mushrooms
½ cup	beer
3 tbsp	Mexican chili powder
1 tsp	ground cumin (preferably freshly toasted and ground)
1 tsp	ground coriander (preferably freshly toasted and ground)
1 tsp	smoked paprika
½ tsp	dried oregano
1	can (19 oz/540 ml) white kidney beans, drained and rinsed
1	can (28 oz/796 ml) whole tomatoes, puréed with an immersion blender
3 cups	peeled and chopped butternut squash (1 small squash)
3 cups	vegetable stock
1 cup	dried small-granule TVP
2 ½ tsp	sea salt

1. Heat oil in a large pot over medium-high heat.
2. Add onion, garlic, and mushrooms and cook until they start to brown, stirring often.
3. Add beer, chili powder, cumin, coriander, paprika, and oregano. Stir and cook for 2 to 3 minutes to cook the spices.
4. Add remaining ingredients, bring to a boil, then reduce heat and simmer until squash is tender.

Thai Tomato with Green Chilies and Kaffir Lime Leaves

Imade this soup one night at home when I thought there was nothing in the house to eat. But I did have a can of tomatoes, a can of coconut milk, some green chilies in the fridge, and kaffir lime leaves in the pantry. As soon as I took the first taste of this soup, I jumped up to get a pen and paper and write down exactly what had gone into it so that I could duplicate it for the restaurant.

Dried kaffir lime leaves are readily available these days, but if you can find fresh ones, use those. The chilies and lime leaves are not meant to be eaten—fish them out before serving the soup, or tell your guests to leave them in their bowls.

Whenever I use canned tomatoes, I use whole ones and purée them myself. To me, the canned chopped tomatoes don't taste quite as good as freshly puréed whole ones.

Serves 6

1 tbsp	olive oil
1	onion, chopped
4	cloves garlic, minced
1	can (28 oz/796 ml) whole tomatoes
1	can (14 oz/400 ml) coconut milk
3 cups	vegetable stock
8	Thai green chilies, halved, or 1 tsp sambal oelek
8	dried kaffir lime leaves

1. Heat oil in a large pot over medium heat.
2. Add onion and garlic and sauté for 2 to 3 minutes, until softened.
3. Add tomatoes and coconut milk. Purée with an immersion blender until just a few chunks of tomatoes remain.
4. Add stock, chilies, and lime leaves.
5. Bring to a boil, then reduce heat and simmer for about 20 minutes to infuse soup with the flavour of the chilies and lime leaves.

Salads

Chopped Caesar

Jessica Brousseau, kitchen manager at our Bloor location, loves this salad. It's her favourite thing on the menu, and she sometimes likes to have it in a wrap. To do this, make the salad as directed and put it inside a grilled tortilla.

If you've never used jicama before, don't be afraid. It tastes like a cross between a water chestnut and a potato, and has a great crunch. It's easiest to use a large knife to prep it. The peel has a fibrous layer right under the outer skin, so remove that, then cut the jicama into thin slices, and then the slices into sticks.

This salad is a great combo of creamy, crunchy, sweet, salty, and nutty flavours and textures. At the restaurants, this salad comes in an appetizer size. This recipe is for twice that size, so it's enough for a meal for one person or an appetizer for two.

Serves 1 to 2

2 cups	spring mix salad greens
2 cups	finely sliced napa cabbage
4 tbsp	shelled, ready-to-eat edamame
½ cup	diced red pepper
4 tbsp	Caesar Dressing (page 105)
½ cup	sliced jicama (cut into small sticks)
4 tbsp	sliced sun-dried tomatoes
2 tsp	pine nuts
2 to 3	slices cooked Tempeh Bacon (page 127), sliced thinly on the diagonal (about 3 tbsp)

1. Toss salad greens, cabbage, edamame, and red pepper with dressing and pile into a large serving bowl.

2. Pile jicama in a pyramid shape on top of salad, and sprinkle sun-dried tomatoes, pine nuts, and tempeh on top.

Antioxidant Salad

This salad is chock full of so many antioxidant ingredients, it had to have this name! You can almost feel yourself getting healthier when you eat it. If you don't like the way beet juice stains purple the other vegetables it touches, you can squeeze out most of the juice after you grate them. Put the grated beets in a clean dishcloth (one that you don't mind if it stains from the beet juice), twist the ends together, and squeeze the juice out over the sink. This recipe makes enough for a meal for one.

Serves 1 as a meal

4 cups	baby spinach
¼ cup	shredded carrot
¼ cup	shredded raw beet
¼ cup	chopped red pepper
4	grape tomatoes, halved
1 tbsp	raisins
2 tbsp	House Dressing (page 105)
1 tbsp	coarsely chopped parsley
¼ cup	alfalfa sprouts, pulled apart into strands
1	lemon wedge

1. Toss baby spinach, carrot, beet, red pepper, tomatoes, and raisins with dressing in a large serving bowl.

2. Sprinkle parsley and sprouts on top and serve with a lemon wedge.

Wedge Salad

Iceberg lettuce has fallen out of favour in recent years, but it's fun to embrace its retro charms now and then. Wedge salads are traditionally served with blue cheese dressing and bacon, but I have veganized it by using a vegan creamy, ranch-like dressing and Tempeh Bacon (page 127). This recipe makes more dressing than you'll need for four salads, so use leftovers as a dip for vegetables or on any other salad. Don't be afraid of the long ingredient list in this dressing. It will be worth it, I promise.

Serves 4

Dressing

2 tsp	sunflower oil
½ cup	chopped carrot
¼ cup	diced onion
¼ cup	chopped celery
2	cloves garlic, sliced
⅛ tsp	sea salt
½ cup	vegetable stock
¼ cup	cheddar-style Daiya vegan cheese
2 tbsp	water, plus more as needed
1 tsp	lemon juice
½ tsp	Dijon mustard
2 tbsp	sunflower oil
½ cup	silken tofu
¼ tsp	sea salt
¼ tsp	freshly ground black pepper
¼ cup	chopped parsley
1 tbsp	fresh dill or 1 tsp dried dill
1 tbsp	chopped green onion

Salad

1	head iceberg lettuce
12	slices cooked Tempeh Bacon (page 127) (about 1 cup)
4	radishes, cut into thin slices
½ cup	Protein Boost (page 133)
2 to 4	canned hearts of palm, cut into about 20 slices
16	grape tomatoes, halved

To make dressing:

1. Heat 2 tsp sunflower oil in a frying pan over medium-low heat. Add carrot, onion, celery, garlic, and sea salt. Cook, stirring often, until softened but not browned.
2. Add stock and simmer until carrot is softened and most of liquid has evaporated.
3. Add Daiya cheese and stir until melted.
4. Remove from heat and let cool (to speed this up, transfer the mixture to a bowl and put it in the fridge).
5. Once carrot mixture is cool, put the ingredients in a blender in the following order: water, lemon juice, mustard, 2 tbsp sunflower oil, tofu, sea salt, pepper, carrot mixture, parsley, dill, and green onion. Make sure the liquid is at the bottom of the blender by the blades.
6. Blend until smooth, adding extra water 1 tbsp at a time if needed.
7. Refrigerate until ready to use.

To assemble:

1. Remove outer leaves of lettuce. Cut into 4 wedges and remove cores.
2. Spoon 1 tbsp dressing onto each of 4 plates.
3. Place lettuce on top of dressing and drizzle each wedge with 2 tbsp of dressing.
4. Top each lettuce wedge with Tempeh Bacon and radishes. Sprinkle 2 tbsp Protein Boost over each.
5. Arrange hearts of palm and tomatoes on the plates.

Golden Beet and Apple Salad

I love yellow beets because you get the earthy flavour of beets without having to worry about them leaking their juice all over everything. When roasted, their natural sweetness comes out and really transforms the flavour. Try to find small, golf-ball–sized beets—the big ones can sometimes be a bit woody and fibrous. If you can't find mini yellow tomatoes, which often come packaged along with other mini multi-coloured heirloom varieties, use regular grape tomatoes. Choose your favourite kind of apple for this salad. To cut apples, quarter them first, remove the core then slice.

Serves 2 as an appetizer

1 cup	peeled and thinly sliced yellow beets
1 tsp	sunflower oil
pinch	sea salt
4 cups	baby arugula
5 tsp	House Dressing (page 105)
1 cup	thinly sliced apple
10	mini yellow tomatoes, quartered or halved, depending on size
2 tbsp	Fibre Boost (page 133)

1. Preheat oven to 350°F.
2. Toss sliced beets with sunflower oil and sea salt, making sure to coat all surfaces with oil.
3. Spread beets out on a baking sheet and roast for 10 minutes. Remove from the oven and flip them over, then roast for another 10 minutes or until tender and browned on the edges.
4. Toss arugula with 4 tsp of the dressing and arrange on 2 plates.
5. Top with roasted beets, apple slices, and tomatoes, distributing each ingredient evenly over top of the arugula.
6. Drizzle remaining 1 tsp of dressing over the two salads, and sprinkle each with 1 tbsp of Fibre Boost.

Go Green

This celebration of all things green is a perfect meal to make you feel like you did something good for your insides, but also for your taste buds. It's easy to sneak raw kale into your life if you just shred it up very finely. You could even fool someone who thinks they don't like kale by hiding it among the other leaves in this salad. You can find ready-to-eat shelled edamame in the freezer section of most grocery stores these days. They just need to be thawed then they're ready to eat. If you can't find them, steam or boil raw edamame for 1 minute, then refresh in cold water. There are pistachios in this salad, but if you want a bit more protein, a good sprinkling of Protein Boost (page 133) would be a great addition.

Serves 1 as a meal

1 cup	baby arugula
1 cup	baby spinach
½ cup	finely shredded kale
½ cup	finely sliced napa cabbage
½ cup	chopped avocado
⅓ cup	shelled, ready-to-eat edamame
¼ cup	finely sliced celery, cut on the diagonal
4 to 6 tbsp	Creamy Herb Dressing (page 104)
1 tbsp	chopped pistachios

1. Toss all the ingredients together in a large serving bowl.

Kale and Oyster Mushroom Salad

This salad is my new addiction. Raw kale and baby arugula topped with quick-roasted oyster mushrooms is an easy and impressive salad to make for yourself or for guests.

Those of you who are from Toronto might recognize these mushrooms—they were inspired by the ones on the Funghi Assoluti pizza at Terroni. I really wanted to figure out a way to recreate them in a vegan version, and as soon as I tried them with Brazil nuts, I knew the search was over. It's not a mistake that the kale and arugula is tossed with the dressing before you turn on the oven. You want the kale to marinate, and the time it takes for the oven to heat up to 500°F gives it time to soften up a little.

Serves 2

Salad

4 cups	finely chopped kale
2 cups	baby arugula
2 tbsp	extra-virgin olive oil
2 tsp	balsamic vinegar
¼ tsp	sea salt
pinch	freshly ground black pepper

Vegan Parmesan Coating

2 tbsp	very finely chopped Brazil nuts
2 tbsp	nutritional yeast flakes
2 tbsp	sesame seeds
½ tsp	sea salt

Mushrooms

3 cups	oyster mushrooms, caps separated and large stems removed
3 tbsp	olive oil

Garnishes

1 cup	chopped pea sprouts (optional)
8	grape tomatoes, halved

1. For salad, mix together kale, arugula, olive oil, vinegar, sea salt, and pepper in a large bowl. Massage the mixture with your hands, then set aside, tossing a couple of times while you're preparing the mushrooms.
2. Preheat oven to 500°F.
3. For coating, in a small bowl, mix together Brazil nuts, nutritional yeast, sesame seeds, and sea salt.
4. Toss mushrooms with 3 tbsp olive oil and the coating.
5. Place mushrooms on a baking sheet, gill-side up. Scrape out any coating that is left in the bowl and press it onto the mushrooms.
6. Roast mushrooms for 5 to 7 minutes or until nicely browned.
7. Meanwhile, divide the kale mixture onto 2 plates and garnish with pea sprouts and grape tomatoes.
8. Top each salad with half of the cooked mushrooms.

Good Salad

The original version of this salad is referred to in my family as simply "Good Salad." We had it often when I was growing up, and I've missed it since I went vegetarian, since there's bacon, eggs, and cheese in it. I was very happy to be able to recreate it in a vegan version without losing any of the magic of the original.

Don't be tempted to use store-bought croutons. To make this salad work, the croutons need to be crispy and delectable, so you need to make them yourself, and it's easy to do. If you can't find pea sprouts, use all romaine, or substitute baby arugula or any kind of long-stemmed sprout. To avoid the winged look romaine has when cut straight across the head, tear the leaves into pieces or cut the head into 4 wedges lengthwise and then chop across those.

Serves 4 as an appetizer or 6 as a side dish

Croutons

2 tbsp	olive oil
2 cups	cubed multigrain bread

Dressing

4 tbsp	olive oil
2 tbsp	lemon juice
1	clove garlic, minced
1 tsp	finely chopped fresh oregano
1 tsp	finely chopped fresh mint
¼ tsp	sea salt

Salad

1 cup	diced Tempeh Bacon (page 127), (6 to 12 slices)
6 cups	torn or chopped romaine lettuce
2 cups	chopped pea sprouts
1 cup	grape tomatoes, halved
½ cup	chopped cucumber
2 tbsp	chopped green onion

1. For croutons, heat oil in a frying pan over medium-high heat. Add bread cubes and cook until browned, stirring often. Remove from heat and set aside.
2. Mix together all dressing ingredients in a small bowl.
3. Mix together croutons and salad ingredients in a large serving bowl and toss with dressing.

Eat Your Greens!

This is a very popular salad in the restaurants' retail fridges. The name says it all. We use a combination of baby arugula, baby spinach, and mesclun, but you can use whatever leaves are your favourite.

Serves 1 as a meal

4 cups	mixed salad greens
⅓ cup	diced cucumber
2 tbsp	green peas
2 tbsp	Green Dressing (page 107)
½ cup	sunflower sprouts
4	slices avocado, chopped
2 tsp	toasted pumpkin seeds

1. Toss salad greens, cucumber, and peas with dressing in a large serving bowl.
2. Top with sprouts, avocado, and pumpkin seeds.

Walnut and Asiago Salad

I love the Poppy Seed Dressing on this salad because its sweetness is a perfect foil for the savoury cheese and walnuts.

Serves 1 as a meal

4 cups	mixed salad greens
4	grape tomatoes, halved
3	dried apricots, finely sliced
3 tbsp	finely sliced celery
3 tbsp	chopped toasted walnuts
4 tbsp	Poppy Seed Dressing (page 106)
⅓ cup	finely sliced asiago cheese

1. Toss salad greens, tomatoes, apricots, celery, and walnuts with dressing in a large serving bowl.
2. Top with asiago cheese.

Hazelnut and Goat Cheese Salad

This salad, with its delicious combination of sweet, salty, nutty, and creamy, is a favourite at the restaurants, where it's available in the retail fridges.

Serves 1 as a meal

4 cups	mixed salad greens
2 tbsp	chopped hazelnuts
1 tbsp	currants
2 tbsp	House Dressing (page 105)
3 to 6	slices cooked Tempeh Bacon (page 127), (about ⅓ cup)
4 tbsp	soft goat cheese

1. Toss salad greens, hazelnuts, and currants with dressing in a large serving bowl.
2. Top with tempeh bacon and goat cheese.

Asian Salad

This is one of the salads we sell from the retail fridges at our Bloor and Spadina locations. We use a mix of mesclun, baby spinach, and baby arugula in all our fridge salads. You can use a combination, like we do, or just choose your favourite kind of lettuce or salad greens.

Serves 1 as a meal

4 cups	mixed salad greens
⅓ cup	finely sliced napa cabbage
4 tbsp	Peanut Lime Dressing (page 106)
¼ cup	shredded or spiralized carrots
¼ cup	shredded or spiralized yellow beets
⅓ cup	bean sprouts
½ cup	sunflower sprouts
1 tbsp	chopped peanuts
2	Grilled Tofu Steaks (page 131), sliced

1. Toss salad greens and napa cabbage with 3 tbsp of the dressing and pile into a large serving bowl.
2. Top with remaining ingredients and drizzle the remaining 1 tbsp of dressing over top.

Middle Eastern Salad

My family doesn't live in Toronto, so they don't get to eat Fresh food very often. Last summer I met my mother, sister, and grandmother at the train station on their stopover to Brockville, Ontario, and I brought lunch from Fresh for them to eat on the train. This salad was one of the things I included, and they loved it, even my 91-year-old Nana!

Serves 1 as a meal

4 cups	mixed salad greens
⅓ cup	diced cucumber
⅓ cup	diced tomato
2 tbsp	chopped parsley
1 tbsp	diced red onion
2 to 4 tbsp	Tahini Sauce (page 111)
3 tbsp	Fresh Salad Topper (page 62)
4	cooked Herb Falafel Balls (page 16)

1. Toss salad greens, cucumber, tomato, parsley, and red onion with sauce and pile into a large serving bowl. Start with 2 tbsp of sauce, adding more to taste.
2. Sprinkle Salad Topper over salad and arrange falafel balls on top.

San Francisco Slaw

This salad has lots of different things going on, but they all work perfectly together. Every bite is slightly different and every bite is delicious. This recipe was inspired by a green tea salad I had on my 40th birthday trip to San Francisco. I tried so hard to find the fermented green tea leaves that were in that salad, but it seems that they are not available in Canada. So I took my memories of that salad and reinvented it without the green tea but with the spiciness and freshness of the original. If you can find it, buy living cilantro. It comes in a package with the roots attached and has delicate, tender stems that can be eaten—just cut off the roots.

Serves 2

3 cups	finely sliced napa cabbage
2 tbsp	finely sliced red onion
2 tbsp	olive oil
3	cloves garlic, finely sliced
¼ tsp	sea salt
1 tbsp	freshly squeezed lime juice
2 tbsp	toasted peanuts
1 tsp	sesame seeds
½ tsp	sambal oelek
8	grape tomatoes, quartered
½ cup	chopped pea sprouts
½ cup	chopped cilantro

1. Put napa cabbage and red onion in a large serving bowl.

2. Heat olive oil and garlic in a frying pan over medium heat.

3. As soon as the garlic starts to brown, pour the oil and garlic over the cabbage and onion and toss to mix thoroughly. Add remaining ingredients and toss mixture together. Add more sea salt if needed and serve immediately.

Fresh Slaw

We serve a small portion of this slaw alongside all of our wraps and burgers at the restaurants.

Makes 5 cups

2 cups	finely sliced green cabbage
1 cup	finely sliced red cabbage
1 cup	finely sliced celery
½ cup	finely sliced fennel
½ cup	finely sliced red onion

Dressing

¼ cup	sunflower oil
2 tbsp	rice vinegar
2 tbsp	apple cider vinegar
4 tsp	organic sugar
¼ tsp	dried dill
¼ tsp	Mexican chili powder
¼ tsp	sea salt
⅛ tsp	freshly ground black pepper

1. Toss together cabbages, celery, fennel, and red onion in a large serving bowl.
2. Mix together all dressing ingredients in a small bowl.
3. Pour dressing over vegetables and toss to mix. Serve immediately.

Tangled Thai Salad

At Fresh we use a turning slicer (spiralizer) to cut the carrot and yellow beets into super-long, thin strands that form a big round tangle of a salad. You probably don't have a turning slicer at home, so it's worth getting a julienne peeler, which will give you nice long strands as well. They won't be mega-long, like ours, but a turning slicer is about $100, and a julienne peeler is only about $10, so it's a pretty good compromise. If you don't have either, just cut the vegetables into sticks as thin and long as you can.

Serves 1 as a meal

1 cup	chopped napa cabbage
⅓ cup	sliced jicama (cut into small sticks)
⅔ cup	shredded or spiralized carrot
⅔ cup	shredded or spiralized yellow beet
4 tbsp	Peanut Lime Dressing (page 106)
3	slices cucumber, halved
2 tsp	chopped raw peanuts
2 tbsp	Fresh Salad Topper (page 62)
1	lime wedge
2 to 3 tbsp	chopped cilantro

1. Put napa cabbage in a large, shallow serving bowl (or plate). Top with jicama.
2. Pile the carrot and beet on top and drizzle with dressing.
3. Garnish with the cucumber, peanuts, Salad Topper, lime, and cilantro.

Fresh Salad Topper

This crunchy mix adds great flavour and texture to any salad. If you want to use it as a topper for fruit salad, yogurt, or oatmeal, leave the salt out or replace it with sugar. If you can't find puffed quinoa at your local health food store, you can substitute puffed millet. This mixture keeps for months in an airtight container.

Makes about 1 ¾ cups

1 cup	puffed quinoa
¼ cup	goji berries
¼ cup	currants
2 tbsp	sliced almonds
2 tbsp	chopped hazelnuts
2 tbsp	chopped pistachios
¼ tsp	sea salt

1. Put all the ingredients in a bowl and mix well.

Mâche and Yellow Tomato Salad

This is such a simple salad, you might be surprised how delicious it is. Mâche, also known as lamb's lettuce, has a delicate flavour that would be overpowered by vinegar or lemon juice, so here it is dressed only with olive oil and sea salt. Whenever I sit down with this salad, I think, "This can't possibly be very good, I should add something," but by the time I'm finished eating it, I want to lick the plate. I usually have this salad on its own as an appetizer so that I can really appreciate it. If it were served alongside a flavourful entrée, its subtleties would be lost. If you can't find mâche, use baby arugula instead. It won't be the same, but it will still be delicious. Just keep your eyes out for mâche and when you see it, grab it!

Serves 1 as an appetizer

1 ½ cups	mâche
1	yellow tomato, cut into wedges
¼	yellow pepper, cut into wedges
2 tsp	pine nuts
1 tsp	mild-flavoured olive oil
pinch	sea salt
1 to 2 tbsp	shaved parmesan cheese (optional)

1. Pile mâche on a plate.
2. Arrange the tomato and yellow pepper wedges in a pinwheel pattern on top of the mâche, and sprinkle the pine nuts over top.
3. Drizzle with olive oil and sprinkle with sea salt
4. Garnish with parmesan cheese if using

Sandwiches + Wraps

Goat Cheese and Red Pesto Sandwich

This delicious combination is one of the most popular selections in our retail fridges. This sandwich is great for a picnic because it holds up well—even if made in the morning and not eaten until the afternoon. The recipe for Red Pesto will make ½ cup, and you will only need half of that for the sandwiches, but the pesto keeps for a long time in the fridge, and it is so good that I'm sure you will use it up in no time. Use it on pasta, as a dip for crackers or vegetables, on a pizza, or with anything else you like.

Serves 4

1	white baguette, cut in 4
8 tsp	butter
1	batch Red Pesto (page 110)
½ cup	soft goat cheese
12	slices tomato
	sea salt
	freshly ground black pepper
½ cup	finely sliced red pepper
2 cups	spring mix salad greens

1. Cut each piece of baguette in half lengthwise. Spread each piece with 1 tsp butter.
2. Spread the bottom pieces of baguette with 1 tbsp pesto each.
3. Spread 2 tbsp goat cheese on each baguette bottom. Top each with 3 tomato slices, then sprinkle with salt and pepper to taste.
4. Distribute red pepper and salad greens among baguettes. Add the baguette tops and serve.

Asiago and Grilled Pear Sandwich

This is an enduring favourite in Fresh's retail fridges. The tangy, nutty cheese with the sweet pear and peppery arugula is a great combination.

Serves 4

8 to 12	thin slices ripe pear
1	white baguette, cut in 4
	mayonnaise of your choice
100 g	asiago cheese, finely sliced
2	tomatoes, sliced
	sea salt
	freshly ground black pepper
4 cups	baby arugula

1. Heat a grill pan over high heat. Grill pears until softened and starting to caramelize.
2. Cut each piece of baguette in half lengthwise.
3. Spread each piece of baguette with mayonnaise.
4. Lay cheese in a single layer on 4 bottom pieces of bread.
5. Top with grilled pear and tomato slices.
6. Sprinkle with salt and pepper to taste.
7. Top with baby arugula and bread tops.

Teriyaki Spare Rib Sandwich

When I was a kid, my mum made spare ribs with a sticky sweet soy glaze. Everyone who grew up in the 1970s probably knows the ones I'm talking about. Since I've been vegetarian, I haven't been able to satisfy the craving for those ribs of my childhood. They are the inspiration for this sandwich, and the craving has been totally satisfied, finally! You can use tamari or soy sauce to make the teriyaki sauce, but soy sauce definitely gives more of that retro flavour. Watch out for really cheap soy sauce, because it usually has caramel flavour and other unexpected ingredients in it. Buy better-quality soy sauce made of just soybeans, water, and wheat. Most grocery stores carry pre-made slaw mixes of all kinds: I've seen traditional cabbage slaw everywhere, but increasingly available are other blends, like carrot slaw and broccoli slaw. At Fresh, we use our own slaw mix, but I've been known to buy a pre-made mix for home just for the convenience of it.

Serves 4

1 cup	dried TVP slices
1	batch Teriyaki Sauce (recipe follows)
3 cups	slaw mix (store-bought or Fresh Slaw, page 59)
½ cup	vegan mayonnaise of your choice
1 tsp	lemon juice
1	white or whole-wheat baguette, cut in 4
2 cups	baby arugula
12	thin slices tomato
	sea salt
	freshly ground black pepper
12	thin rings red onion
12	thin rings red pepper

Teriyaki Sauce

¼ cup	organic sugar
3 tbsp	soy sauce
1 tbsp	water
2 tsp	sunflower oil
1 tsp	sesame oil
1 tsp	grated ginger
1	clove garlic, minced

1. Bring 3 or 4 cups of water to a boil in a small pot. Turn off heat and add TVP. Stir, then let sit for 15 or 20 minutes to rehydrate. Drain.

2. Meanwhile, make teriyaki sauce. Combine all sauce ingredients in a bowl, stirring well to dissolve the sugar.

3. Add rehydrated TVP to sauce and stir to coat. Transfer to a large frying pan set over high heat and spread out in a single layer.

4. Let the teriyaki sauce start to boil away. When the sauce is almost all evaporated, reduce heat to medium and let the slices cook until they are deep brown and caramelized on both sides, turning with tongs or a fork, and watching closely so they don't burn. Transfer to a plate to cool.

5. Put slaw mix in a bowl and toss with mayonnaise and lemon juice.

6. Cut each piece of baguette in half lengthwise. Scoop out some of the bread from the top section of each piece of baguette to make room for the filling.

7. Divide slaw mix among the 4 top pieces of baguette.

8. On bottom pieces of baguette, place arugula and then TVP slices. Top with tomato and sprinkle with salt and pepper to taste. Add onion and red pepper slices.

9. Put tops and bottoms together and serve.

BBQ Tempeh Sandwich

Meghan Pike, kitchen manager at our Spadina location, is the queen of making the sandwiches for our retail fridges. She can make 50 assorted sandwiches in 1 hour!

Serves 4

1	batch uncooked BBQ Tempeh (page 132)
	canola oil, for cooking
8	slices multigrain bread
½ cup	vegan mayonnaise of your choice
2 tsp	Dijon mustard
4 cups	spring mix salad greens
16	slices tomato
	sea salt
	freshly ground black pepper
8	slices dill pickle
16	thin rings red onion

1. Grill or pan-fry tempeh with a little canola oil, flipping to brown on both sides. Set aside to cool.
2. Spread each piece of bread with mayonnaise, then spread mustard on 4 of the pieces.
3. Arrange salad greens on 4 of the pieces of bread, top with tomato slices, and sprinkle with salt and pepper to taste.
4. Divide tempeh, dill pickle, and red onion among sandwiches, and top with remaining slices of bread. Cut in half diagonally.

BBQ Tempeh and Aged Cheddar Sandwich

At Fresh, we sell two versions of this sandwich in our retail fridges: on demi-baguettes and on multigrain bread. You can make these either way, depending on which kind of bread you like. This sandwich keeps well—great for a packed lunch, and kids love them. We make both vegan and non-vegan versions. For the vegan version, BBQ Tempeh Sandwich, see page 69. In this version we use extra-old cheddar cut super thin with a cheese plane, to get maximum flavour with a minimum amount.

Serves 4

1	batch uncooked BBQ Tempeh (page 132)
	canola oil, for cooking
4	demi-baguettes or 1 regular baguette cut in 4
½ cup	mayonnaise of your choice
4 cups	mixed salad greens
16	slices tomato
	sea salt
	freshly ground black pepper
12	thin slices extra-old cheddar cheese
16	slices cucumber

1. Grill or pan-fry tempeh in a little canola oil, flipping to brown on both sides. Set aside to cool.

2. Cut baguettes in half lengthwise and spread both sides with mayonnaise.

3. Distribute salad greens on bottom halves of baguette, top with tomato slices, and sprinkle with salt and pepper to taste.

4. Divide cheese, tempeh, and cucumber among baguettes. Put on baguette tops and serve.

Tempeh BLT Sandwich

My first cooking memory is of bacon. I can't remember how old I was, but my mum was cooking bacon in a pan and she asked me to watch it while she went upstairs to do something. So I stood there and watched it. I watched it and watched it while it turned into black lumps in the pan. When my mum came back, she said, "I asked you to watch the bacon!" and I said, "I did!" It never occurred to me to do anything else but watch it. Who would ever have thought that I would end up cooking for a living!

Sometimes you crave this classic combo, even if you don't eat meat anymore. The Tempeh Bacon captures the smoky, salty, savoury goodness of bacon. You could bulk up this sandwich with avocado, cheese, onion, or whatever you like, but the original trio is all you really need. It's a classic for a reason.

Serves 1

2	slices multigrain bread
2 tbsp	vegan mayonnaise of your choice
1 or 2	romaine lettuce leaves
4	slices cooked Tempeh Bacon (page 127)
4	slices tomato
	sea salt
	freshly ground black pepper

1. Toast bread and spread one side of each slice with mayonnaise.
2. Lay lettuce leaves on one slice of toast.
3. Place tempeh slices and then tomato on top of lettuce.
4. Sprinkle tomatoes with sea salt and pepper to taste.
5. Top with remaining piece of toast, cut in half, and serve.

Portobello Pesto Sandwich

The pesto recipe makes twice as much as you need for these sandwiches, so make half a batch only or make the whole batch and you'll have some pesto to use for the Italian Raw Bowl (page 90).

Serves 4

4 to 8	Portobello mushrooms (1 per sandwich if large, 2 if small)
2 tsp	tamari
2 tsp	olive oil
4	whole-wheat buns
1	batch Pesto (page 109)
4 cups	spring mix salad greens
1 cup	alfalfa sprouts

1. Preheat oven to 400°F.
2. Clean mushrooms. Remove stems and discard.
3. Mix tamari with olive oil in a large bowl.
4. Toss mushroom caps in oil mixture, making sure all surfaces are coated.
5. Lay mushroom caps on a baking sheet, gill-side up, and roast for 7 to 10 minutes or until tender.
6. Toast buns and spread each side with 1 tbsp pesto.
7. On bottom half of each bun, arrange 1 cup of salad greens, 1 or 2 mushroom caps, and ¼ cup alfalfa sprouts.
8. Put on bun tops.

Greek Pita

Years ago I was stuck on Santorini for a week when windstorms made it too dangerous for ferries to leave the island. *Stuck* on Santorini, you say? Well, it felt like it because we had to fight our way through sand clouds whenever we were outside. Plus, my boyfriend and I were on the verge of breaking up, and we were staying in a hotel that cost only about $10 a night, so you can imagine that hanging out in the room wasn't much fun. Food became very important during that week. Down the street was a little stand that sold souvlaki in a pita, and we ended up having it for lunch and dinner almost every day. The pitas were crispy and savoury, and I couldn't figure out how the cook made them so delicious, so I finally asked him, and he showed me his simple method.

Make these pitas the traditional way, with tzatziki and feta, or try one of the vegan versions: vegan with tofu, or vegan with cauliflower. All are delicious; decide which to make based on what you have in the fridge or dietary requirements. You can also add sautéed meatless "chicken" tenders for more protein. If you're making a few and have a large flat-top griddle, prepare them all at the same time. Or prepare them one at a time in a frying pan. You can keep the pitas warm in the oven, to serve all at once, but the pitas are crispier if served right after removing them from the pan.

Serves 4

5 tsp	canola oil
4	Greek-style pitas
2 tsp	paprika
2 tsp	garlic powder
¾ cup	store-bought tzatziki or 1 batch Vegan Tzatziki (recipe follows)
½ cup	crumbled feta cheese or 1 batch Tofu Ricotta (recipe follows) or Cauliflower Feta (recipe follows)
1 cup	chopped cucumber
1 cup	chopped tomato
1 cup	shredded iceberg lettuce
¼ cup	chopped red onion

To prepare pitas:

1. Preheat oven to 200°F, if you plan to keep pitas warm as the others cook.
2. Heat 1 tsp oil in a frying pan over medium-high heat.
3. Sprinkle one side of a pita with ¼ tsp each of paprika and garlic powder. Rub it into the surface of the pita with your fingers.
4. Place pita in pan, spiced-side down. Sprinkle the other side with another ¼ tsp each of paprika and garlic powder, rubbing it in.
5. Let cook for 1 or 2 minutes, until pita is crispy. Turn over and cook the other side. If pan seems too dry, add a little more oil when cooking the second side.
6. Repeat Steps 3 to 5 with each pita, wiping pan out with a cloth or paper towel between each one.
7. As each pita is done, place on baking sheet and keep warm in oven, or assemble (see below) and serve right away.

To assemble:

1. Lay out a square of foil, a couple of inches wider than the pita on each side.
2. Lay pita on foil, with the "top" edge of pita hanging very slightly over the foil.
3. Vertically down the centre of the pita, put one-quarter of the tzatziki, feta, cucumber, tomato, lettuce, and onion.
4. Use the foil to roll the pita up as tight as you can get it by pulling the two sides together and then folding up the bottom edge to form a package.
5. Repeat with remaining pitas.
6. To eat, just unroll the foil as you go.

Vegan Tzatziki

Serves 4

½ cup	Tofutti sour cream
¼ cup	finely diced cucumber
1	clove garlic, minced
½ tsp	dried dill
¼ tsp	sea salt

1. Stir all ingredients together in a bowl and let sit for a few minutes for flavours to develop.

Tofu Ricotta

Serves 4

2	cloves garlic
2 cups	chopped firm tofu
3 tbsp	olive oil
2 tbsp	lemon juice
1 tsp	miso
½ tsp	sea salt
¼ tsp	dried rosemary

1. Mince garlic in a food processor.
2. Add remaining ingredients and pulse until garlic and tofu are finely chopped but not puréed. Scrape down sides of processor with a spatula a couple of times during processing.

Cauliflower Feta

Serves 4

2 cups	chopped cauliflower
3 tbsp	olive oil
½ tsp	sea salt
½ tsp	miso

1. In a food processor, pulse cauliflower with oil, sea salt, and miso until cauliflower is minced but not puréed—a few seconds. Scrape down sides of processor with a spatula if needed.

Sam Houston Burrito

y dad was an athlete when he was younger. He was drafted by the Ottawa Roughriders and scouted by the Dallas Cowboys but was sidelined by an injury before he could play. Two nicknames have followed him since those days—Tex and Sam, both because of our last name. I always loved those names, and I ended up naming my cat Tex and my bulldog Sam. I thought this burrito, with its Southwest, Tex-Mex–inspired flavours, was a perfect one to be named after both of my Sam Houstons.

Makes 6 medium wraps

Taco Seasoning
1 tbsp	Mexican chili powder
1 ½ tsp	ground cumin
¾ tsp	garlic powder
¾ tsp	onion powder
1 tsp	paprika
1 tsp	freshly ground black pepper
½ tsp	sea salt
¼ tsp	crushed dried chilies
¼ tsp	oregano

TVP Mix
2 cups	vegetable stock
1 cup	dried small-granule TVP
¼ cup	canola oil
1 cup	finely diced onion
3	cloves garlic, minced
½ cup	peeled and finely diced sweet potato

Wraps
1 tsp	canola oil
1	large green pepper, seeded and cut into ½-inch-thick slices (about 2 cups)
1	large red pepper, seeded and cut into ½-inch-thick slices (about 2 cups)
½	large white onion, cut into ½-inch-thick slices (about 2 cups)
6	8-inch whole-wheat tortillas or the largest ones you can find
1 ½ cups	shredded iceberg lettuce
¾ cup	salsa (store-bought or homemade, see page 110)
1	avocado, cut into 12 slices

To make taco seasoning:

1. Combine all seasoning ingredients in small bowl.

To make TVP mix:

1. Bring 1 cup of the stock to a boil in a small saucepan. Turn off heat and add TVP. Stir, then let sit for a few minutes while TVP rehydrates.
2. In a large saucepan, heat ¼ cup canola oil over medium-high heat.
3. Add onion and cook until just starting to brown.
4. Add garlic, sweet potato, and taco seasoning. Cook for 1 minute, stirring constantly so spices don't stick to the pan and burn. Add rehydrated TVP and remaining stock. Stir, then bring to a boil. Reduce heat to low and simmer for 10 minutes or until sweet potato is softened. Remove from heat.

To make wraps:

1. In a large sauté pan or wok, heat 1 tsp canola oil over high heat. Add peppers and onion. Cook over high heat, tossing occasionally. You want the vegetables to be slightly charred on the sides but still crunchy.
2. Heat tortillas. (You can do this in the toaster by sliding half of the tortilla into the toaster, then, once it is hot, flipping it, watching that the centre doesn't burn. Or heat on a grill, in a frying pan, or in the oven or microwave.)
3. Scatter some lettuce, TVP mix, and peppers and onion down the centre of each tortilla.
4. Top each with 2 tbsp of salsa and 2 avocado slices.
5. Fold edges in and roll up. Cut each in half and serve.

Sam Houston Enchiladas

This recipe can easily be used for enchiladas. Make all 6 wraps without the lettuce and avocado. Lay them side by side in a baking dish. Mix 2 cups of your favourite tomato sauce with 1 cup of salsa and pour over the wraps. Cover with cheese (if using vegan cheese, make sure to use the kind that melts). Bake in a 350°F oven for 20 to 30 minutes or until cheese is melted and wraps are heated through. Serve with avocado slices, and use the lettuce as a side salad, with a dash of lime juice and olive oil, and a sprinkle of salt, for a dressing.

Sunflower Sandwich

Years ago, when I lived in Kingston, Ontario, there was a vegetarian restaurant called The Sunflower, which made a sandwich very much like this one. The restaurant is long gone, but I have never forgotten this sandwich. You might think it's strange to put alfalfa under the broiler, but trust me, it's amazing. The amounts in this recipe are flexible because how much you need depends on how big the slice of bread is.

Serves 1

1 piece	rye bread (or bread of your choice)
2 tsp	mayonnaise of your choice
½ tsp	Dijon mustard
4	slices tomato (or enough to cover bread)
pinch	sea salt
pinch	freshly ground black pepper
4 to 6	thin slices red onion
½ to 1 cup	alfalfa sprouts
4 to 6	slices finely sliced extra-old cheddar or meltable vegan cheese (just enough to cover sprouts)
1 tsp	raw sunflower seeds

1. Preheat broiler.
2. Toast the bread, then spread one side with mayonnaise and mustard.
3. Put tomato slices on top and sprinkle with salt and pepper to taste.
4. Arrange onion slices on top of tomatoes and top with alfalfa.
5. Cover alfalfa with cheese and scatter sunflower seeds on top.
6. Broil until cheese is melted and sunflower seeds are browned. Watch carefully so the seeds don't burn.

Banh Mi

Banh Mi is a Vietnamese sandwich made with a baguette, invented during the French colonization of Vietnam. It traditionally includes daikon, but I tried it with regular red radishes as well, in case you can't find daikon. It wasn't as pungent or authentic-tasting, but it was still really good. Banh Mi also typically gets a drizzle of soy sauce, but in this version I've used tamari, cooked right into the tofu and mushrooms. I like Banh Mi on a bun with a crispy crust and an airy centre that practically disappears when you press the sandwich together. Almost any grocery store will have a bun that fits the bill; you don't have to go anywhere special for it—just make sure the outside crackles when pressed down on. The sandwich won't be the same without that crispy crust.

Serves 4

Marinated Tofu

4 tbsp	canola oil
2 cups	sliced mushrooms
8	cloves garlic, minced
2 tbsp	tamari
2 tsp	sesame oil
1 tsp	freshly ground black pepper
1	block (12 oz/350 g) firm tofu, sliced ¼ inch thick

Marinated Vegetables

½ cup	agave nectar
2 tsp	sea salt
½ cup	white vinegar
2 cups	julienned carrots
2 cups	julienned daikon

Sandwich

4	large crusty whole-wheat buns
¼ to ½ cup	vegan mayonnaise of your choice
16 to 20	slices cucumber
4	sprigs cilantro
	sliced jalapeño pepper or Sriracha hot sauce (optional)

To make marinated tofu:

1. Heat canola oil in pan over medium heat.
2. Add mushrooms and cook until starting to brown.
3. Stir in garlic, tamari, sesame oil, and pepper.
4. Add tofu slices, pushing mushrooms out of the way so the tofu touches the pan.
5. Cook tofu 1 or 2 minutes on each side, making sure each slice is coated with tamari mixture.
6. Remove from heat, let cool, then transfer to a shallow bowl or baking dish to marinate in the fridge for at least 1 hour.

To make marinated vegetables:

1. In a large bowl, combine agave nectar and sea salt.
2. Add vinegar, mixing well.
3. Stir in carrots and daikon and set aside for at least 1 hour and up to 8 hours or overnight, stirring once or twice.

To assemble:

1. Pour the carrot mixture into a strainer to drain off excess marinade.
2. Cut each bun in half and spread each side with mayonnaise.
3. Layer tofu on bottom pieces of bun. Top with cucumber slices, carrot mixture, cilantro, and jalapeño.
4. Put bun top on, squish sandwich together, and serve.

Entrées

Avocado Bowl

This is a very simple bowl that you can whip up in no time at all, especially if the rice is cooked already. It is a perfect example of the formula for a Fresh Bowl, which is rice or soba, a sauce, a protein, vegetables, and accents. In this case, the sauce is the tamari/olive oil and herb mixture; the protein is the chickpeas; the vegetables are onion, avocado, tomatoes, and sprouts; and the accents are almonds and lemon. You can use this formula to invent bowls using your favourite ingredients, and you can make it as complicated or as simple as you like.

Serves 1

1 ½ to 2 cups	cooked brown basmati rice
3 tbsp	Beach Sauce (page 103)
¼ cup	chickpeas
6	grape tomatoes, halved
½	avocado, sliced or chopped
½ cup	sunflower sprouts
½ cup	chopped pea sprouts
2 tbsp	chopped red onion
2 tbsp	sliced almonds or nuts of your choice
2	lemon wedges

1. Put rice in a large serving bowl.
2. Drizzle 1½ tbsp of the Beach Sauce over the rice.
3. Top rice with chickpeas, tomatoes, avocado, sunflower and pea sprouts, and onion.
4. Scatter almonds over top. Drizzle with remaining 1½ tbsp of Beach Sauce.
5. Serve with lemon wedges.

Lemon Udon With Greens

Yum! Lemony, garlicky, and spicy. I love pastas with a clear or brothy sauce that have a lot of taste, and this is one of my favourites. It's perfect on a hot summer day or on a drizzly winter night. This recipe makes enough for two people if it's all you're having, or for four if you're having an appetizer first and dessert afterward.

Serves 2 to 4

2 tbsp	olive oil
2 cups	chopped tomatoes
2 tbsp	minced garlic
2 tsp	lemon zest
2 tsp	sambal oelek
1 tsp	dried oregano
2 cups	vegetable stock
4 cups	chopped mixed leafy greens (e.g., dandelion, kale, Swiss chard)
½ tsp	sea salt
1	pkg (8 oz/230 g) kamut udon noodles, cooked according to package directions
4 tsp	raw pumpkin seeds

1. Heat oil in a large frying pan or wok over medium-high heat.
2. Add tomatoes and garlic. Cook for 1 or 2 minutes, until fragrant.
3. Stir in lemon zest, sambal oelek, and oregano.
4. Add stock and mixed greens, increase the heat to high and cook for 1 or 2 minutes, until the greens are tender-crisp.
5. Add sea salt and cooked noodles, tossing to mix.
6. Transfer to 2 large bowls and sprinkle 2 tsp pumpkin seeds over each.

Gill's Rice Bowl

Gillian Mountney, our area kitchen manager, is constantly coming into the office with delicious concoctions that she makes up on the fly. She says she doesn't mind when I ask for a bite, but I think she does, so now I just wait until she's full and then finish her leftovers. This is one of the best ones she's come up with. Three wedges of lemon might seem like a lot, but you want this one to be quite lemony.

Serves 1

½ cup	chopped broccoli
1 ½ cups	cooked brown basmati rice
2 tbsp	Beach Sauce (page 103)
½	avocado, sliced
⅓ cup	finely sliced napa cabbage
¼ cup	julienned jicama
¼ cup	shredded or spiralized carrot
¼ cup	shredded or spiralized yellow beet
1 tbsp	sliced green onion
2 tbsp	sliced almonds
3	lemon wedges

1. Steam broccoli until crisp tender.
2. Put rice in a large bowl.
3. Drizzle 1 tbsp of the Beach Sauce over rice.
4. Arrange avocado slices on rice and top with napa cabbage, then the broccoli, jicama, carrot, and beet.
5. Top with green onion, almonds, and remaining 1 tbsp of Beach Sauce.
6. Serve with lemon wedges.

Grounding Greens Bowl

If you haven't been eating your vegetables lately and need to get yourself back down to earth with an infusion of greens, try this bowl. If you would like to add more protein to it, add a couple of Grilled Tofu Steaks (page 131). Twelve cups of greens for two people might seem like a lot, but don't worry, it cooks down to a reasonable portion.

Serves 2

3	cloves garlic
	ice water
1 tbsp	olive oil
½ cup	vegetable stock
2 tbsp	Earth Balance or butter
2 tsp	lemon juice
½ tsp	tamari
	sea salt
	freshly ground black pepper
12 cups	chopped mixed leafy greens (e.g., dandelion, kale, Swiss chard)
2 cups	cooked brown basmati rice
1	avocado, chopped
2 tbsp	Protein Boost (page 133)
2 tbsp	chopped walnuts

1. Bring 1 cup of water to a boil in a small saucepan.
2. Add whole cloves of garlic. After 30 seconds, transfer garlic to a small bowl of ice water to cool. Once cool, slice thinly.
3. Combine oil and garlic in small saucepan and cook over medium heat until garlic begins to brown, about 2 minutes.
4. Add stock, bring to a boil, and cook until reduced by half, 5 to 10 minutes.
5. Reduce heat to low. Whisk in Earth Balance, a little at a time, until fully incorporated into the garlic glaze.
6. Add lemon juice, tamari, and sea salt and pepper to taste. Remove pot from heat and set aside.
7. Put some water in a large frying pan or wok over high heat. (If greens are still damp, you will only need about ¼ cup. If they are dry, use ½ cup.)
8. Add greens and cover. Let steam, stirring often, for a few minutes or until greens are tender. Ideally, when the greens are perfectly tender, the water will all have boiled away. If the water is gone and your greens aren't done, add more water. If the greens are done and you still have water, drain it off.
9. Remove pan from heat, add garlic glaze to the greens, and toss to mix well.
10. Scoop 1 cup of rice into each of 2 bowls, top each with half of the greens, half of the avocado, and 1 tbsp each of Protein Boost and walnuts.

Last-Minute Noodles

These noodles are so quick to make, especially if you already have the Omega Shake and Beach Sauce prepared, that you really can make them at the last minute. They are delicious hot or cold. If you don't like spicy food, leave out the sambal oelek. The avocado and pea sprouts are my favourite accents here, but you could add any other vegetables you have on hand. Frozen green peas, grated carrot, shredded napa cabbage, green onions, celery—any of these would be fine, just take a look in your fridge to see what you have. Cooked rice or quinoa can be substituted for the noodles.

Serves 2 to 4

1	pkg (8 oz/230 g) soba or kamut udon noodles
¼ cup	Beach Sauce (page 103), plus more as needed
1 to 3 tbsp	sambal oelek
1 cup	chopped pea sprouts
1	avocado, chopped
3 tbsp	Omega Shake (page 133) or nut or seed of your choice

1. Bring plenty of water to a boil in a large pot.
2. Add noodles and stir until water comes back to a boil. Cook until tender, stirring often.
3. While noodles cook, combine Beach Sauce and sambal oelek to taste in a large bowl.
4. Just before noodles are done, add pea sprouts to pot and cook for a few seconds.
5. Drain noodles and sprouts and add to bowl with Beach Sauce mixture. Toss to mix. Add a bit more sauce if the noodles seem too dry.
6. Transfer noodles to individual bowls and top with avocado and Omega Shake.

Laksa Rice

This recipe was created by Megan Carriere, the kitchen manager at our Crawford location. It is a great way to use up leftover Curry Laksa broth. Feel free to use whatever vegetables you have on hand. This recipe uses broccoli and mixed leafy greens, but you could use asparagus, spinach, zucchini, or any other green vegetable.

Serves 1

1 cup	Curry Laksa broth (page 36)
1 cup	chopped broccoli, cut quite small
1 cup	mixed leafy greens (e.g., bok choy, kale, Swiss chard)
1 cup	cooked brown rice
¼ cup	canned brown lentils, drained and rinsed
¼ cup	chopped tomato
1 tsp	tamari
1 tbsp	chopped green onion
½ tsp	sesame seeds

1. In a large frying pan or wok, heat broth over high heat and boil for 2 or 3 minutes, until it starts to thicken.
2. Add broccoli and mixed greens, cover the pan with a lid, and let the vegetables steam for 1 or 2 minutes, until vegetables are almost tender.
3. Stir in rice, lentils, tomato, and tamari. Reduce heat to medium-high and cook, stirring constantly, until heated through.
4. Transfer to a large bowl and garnish with green onion and sesame seeds.

Italian Raw Bowl

The summer we served this as a special, it became our most successful special ever, selling over 1,000 in a month. It is raw and gluten-free. The dehydrated kale chips are available in most health food stores these days, and add a parmesan-like quality to this dish, but if you can't find them, don't worry, it's still great without them. The pesto recipe makes enough for about five or six of these bowls, depending on how much pesto you put on the noodles. Keep in mind that if you use the Sun-Blushed Tomatoes, this dish won't be totally raw.

Serves 1

1	medium zucchini
2 to 3 tbsp	Pesto (page 109)
4	sun-dried or Sun-Blushed Tomatoes (page 134), sliced
½ cup	grape tomatoes, halved
¼ cup	dehydrated kale chips (optional)
2 tbsp	raw cashews
1 tsp	raw pine nuts

1. Cut zucchini into long, thin strips that resemble noodles with a turning slicer, peeler, or knife. You should end up with about 2 cups.

2. In a mixing bowl, toss zucchini noodles with 2 tbsp of the pesto. Add remaining 1 tbsp if the noodles seem too dry.

3. Transfer noodles to a serving bowl and top with remaining ingredients.

Tiger Noodles

These noodles are delicious hot or cold, and they are still great after sitting a couple of days in the fridge. You might not find that out, though, because you'll probably end up eating them all right away—they are that delicious! The flavoured oil lasts in the fridge for weeks when kept in a tightly closed container Don't remove the pieces of ginger and lemon grass and other aromatics or the flavour will fade. Just strain out the oil you need and put any bits back into the jar.

Stephanie Weinz, manager at our Crawford location, and I are always on a quest for our next "miracle meal"—one where every element is perfect and is exactly what we feel like eating at that moment. These noodles are our latest miracle meal.

Serves 2 to 4, with lots of oil left over

Flavoured Oil

4 cups	sunflower oil
½ cup	coarsely chopped garlic
½ cup	coarsely chopped ginger
2 tbsp	halved red Thai chilies
1 tsp	whole cloves
4	stalks lemon grass, smashed with the back of a knife and sliced on the diagonal
4	star anise
5	kaffir lime leaves

Noodles

1	pkg (8 oz/230 g) noodles of your choice (e.g., soba, kamut udon)
1 cup	frozen green peas
2 tbsp	tamari
1 cup	baby arugula or spinach
1 cup	finely sliced celery
½ cup	whole toasted cashews
⅛ tsp	sea salt
⅛ tsp	freshly ground black pepper

1. For flavoured oil, put all ingredients in a saucepan and bring to a boil over medium heat. (Don't be tempted to put it over high heat, as it might get too hot and burn.) Reduce heat to low and let simmer for about 20 minutes, stirring occasionally. Turn off heat and allow oil to cool.

2. For noodles, cook according to package directions. In the last minute of cooking, add green peas. Drain.

3. Stir flavoured oil well, then ladle ½ cup through a fine mesh strainer into a measuring cup. Add tamari to the oil in the measuring cup and stir. Put spices and other aromatics caught in the strainer back into remaining oil.

4. Put baby arugula in a large bowl.

5. Pour hot noodles and peas on top of arugula. Add the ½ cup strained oil, celery, cashews, sea salt, and pepper.

6. Toss everything together and serve.

Spicy Noodles with Greens and Tofu Ricotta Fritters

I find that canned whole tomatoes taste better than those already crushed or chopped, so I always buy them whole and purée them myself. This sauce is quite spicy. If you don't like spice, use fewer chili flakes. This sauce is very easy to make, so you can make it right when you need it, or make a double batch and freeze it to have on hand.

Serves 4
Makes 2 cups sauce

2 tbsp	olive oil
1 tsp	chili flakes
1	can (28 oz/796 ml) whole tomatoes, puréed with an immersion blender
3	cloves garlic, minced
½ tsp	sea salt
1	pkg (8 oz/230 g) kamut udon noodles or pasta of your choice
	sunflower oil, for frying
1	batch Tofu Ricotta Fritters (page 135)
3 cups	coarsely chopped green kale

1. Heat olive oil in a saucepan over medium-high heat and add chili flakes. As soon as the chilies start to darken, stir in tomatoes.
2. Add garlic and sea salt.
3. Bring mixture to a boil, then reduce heat to medium and let cook until thickened, about 20 or 30 minutes, stirring occasionally.
4. While sauce is cooking, bring plenty of water to a boil in a large pot. Add noodles and stir until the water comes back to a boil. Let cook, stirring occasionally.
5. Heat sunflower oil in a frying pan and start cooking the tofu fritters according to recipe.
6. When the noodles are almost done, add kale to the pot of noodles. When noodles and greens are tender, drain and toss with tomato sauce.
7. Divide noodles among 4 individual bowls and top each with 3 fritters.

British Curry Bowl

I love a traditional Indian or Thai curry as much as the next person, but a British-style curry holds a place in my heart, since it's the kind I grew up with. It is perfect comfort food for me, especially when it's eaten while watching *Coronation Street*, but that's just me! Curry has been made in Britain as far back as the late 1800s, when *Mrs Beeton's Book of Household Management* and other Victorian cookbooks popularized it. Back then, the ingredients that went into a fresh curry paste were not widely available outside India, so cooks depended on curry powder. This version uses TVP slices as the protein component, but if you can't find those, try meatless "chicken" pieces or even cooked chickpeas or white kidney beans. You can use whatever kind of vegetables you like to make up the 10 cups. It's a great way to use up the leftover bits and pieces in your fridge. Serve over brown or white basmati rice.

Serves 4 to 6

4 cups	vegetable stock
2 cups	dried TVP slices
¼ cup	olive oil
2	onions, chopped
5	cloves garlic, minced
3 tbsp	curry powder
¼ cup	spelt flour
2	apples, peeled, cored, and chopped
10 cups	chopped mixed vegetables (e.g., squash, sweet potato, cauliflower, mushrooms, zucchini, carrot, peppers)
¼ cup	raisins
1 tsp	sea salt

1. Bring stock to a boil in a medium saucepan. Turn off heat and add TVP. Stir, then let sit while TVP rehydrates.
2. Heat oil in a large pot over medium-high heat.
3. Add onions and garlic and cook until softened and starting to brown.
4. Add curry powder and cook, stirring constantly, for 1 minute.
5. Add flour and cook, stirring, for 1 minute.
6. Using a ladle, add stock and TVP gradually, stirring constantly, until all stock is incorporated.
7. Stir in apples, mixed vegetables, raisins, and sea salt, and bring to a boil. Reduce heat and simmer for about 30 minutes or until vegetables are done to your liking.
8. Taste and add more salt if needed.

Quinoa, Mushroom, and Asparagus Bowl

This is as delicious as it is healthy. You will feel nicely full after this, not weighed down.

Serves 1

½ cup	quinoa
¾ cup	vegetable stock
1 tsp	olive oil
1 cup	sliced mushrooms
1 cup	2-inch pieces asparagus
½	lemon
¼	avocado, sliced
pinch	sea salt
1 tbsp	sliced almonds
1 tsp	flax or pumpkin oil

1. Rinse quinoa and drain through a fine mesh strainer.
2. Put quinoa in a pot or rice cooker along with the stock. Bring to a boil, reduce heat, and simmer until all water is absorbed.
3. When the quinoa is cooked, heat olive oil in a large frying pan over high heat.
4. Add mushrooms and spread in a single layer so each mushroom is touching the bottom of the pan. Let them cook without moving them too much, until golden brown on the edges, then flip them over using tongs or a fork.
5. Let the mushrooms cook for about 1 minute, then add asparagus and squeeze the juice from the lemon into the pan.
6. Stir the mixture, and as soon as the asparagus starts to char on the edges, remove the pan from the heat.
7. Transfer quinoa to a large bowl. Top with the mushrooms and asparagus.
8. Arrange slices of avocado on top and sprinkle with sea salt. Sprinkle on almonds and drizzle the flax oil over top.

To roast the vegetables

To roast the vegetables rather than pan-frying, preheat oven to 400°F. Toss mushrooms in a bowl with 1 tsp olive oil and spread on a baking sheet. Put in the oven to roast. After 10 minutes, toss asparagus with 1 tsp oil and add to the mushrooms. Stir everything together on the sheet. Return to oven for another 5 to 10 minutes, until asparagus is tender. Remove from oven, squeeze lemon juice over top, and add to quinoa in a serving bowl.

Thanksgiving Dinner

Sometimes you really just want the classic combo of protein, potato, veggies, and gravy, even though you don't eat meat anymore. Every element in this dinner is delicious in its own right, and is, I dare say, better than a traditional turkey dinner. There are two options: pecan-crusted tempeh and roasted Portobello mushrooms (see page 98 for recipes). You can choose one or do both, either way is great. Prepare as much as you can ahead of time so it's not too chaotic. Marinate the tempeh the night before, then coat with pecans in the morning and keep in the fridge until ready to use. Make the gravy and glaze ahead of time and reheat when you're ready to eat.

Serves 4

Roasted Vegetables

4	cloves garlic, minced
4 tbsp	olive oil
½ tsp	sea salt
1 ½ cups	coarsely chopped parsnips, peeled
1 ½ cups	coarsely chopped carrots, peeled
1 ½ cups	chopped celery (cut into large chunks)
2 ½ cups	chopped cauliflower (cut into large chunks)
1 ½ cups	thickly sliced leeks, white part only
1 ½ cups	halved Brussels sprouts (root end and loose leaves discarded)

1. Preheat oven to 400°F.
2. In a large bowl, combine garlic, olive oil, and sea salt.
3. Add vegetables and toss to coat.
4. Spread vegetables on a baking sheet and roast for 15 minutes.
5. Remove from oven and stir.
6. Return to oven for 15 minutes, or until vegetables are tender and browned on the edges.
7. Remove from oven and toss immediately in Vegetable Glaze (recipe follows) to coat.

Vegetable Glaze

3	cloves garlic
	ice water
1 tbsp	olive oil
1	sprig fresh rosemary
½ cup	vegetable stock
2 tbsp	Earth Balance or butter
2 tsp	lemon juice
	sea salt
	freshly ground black pepper

1. Bring 1 cup water to a boil in a small saucepan.
2. Add whole cloves of garlic. After 30 seconds, transfer garlic to a small bowl of ice water to cool. Once cool, slice thinly.
3. Combine oil, garlic, and rosemary in a small pan and cook over medium heat until garlic begins to brown, about 2 minutes.
4. Add stock, bring to a boil, and cook until reduced by half, about 5 to 10 minutes.
5. Discard rosemary.
6. Reduce heat to low. Whisk in Earth Balance, a little at a time, until fully incorporated.
7. Add lemon juice, and sea salt and pepper to taste.
8. Remove from heat and toss with roasted vegetables as soon as they come out of the oven.

Mashed Sweet Potato

6 cups	peeled and chopped sweet potato
2 tbsp	Earth Balance or butter
4 tbsp	unsweetened, unflavoured rice milk
¼ tsp	sea salt
¼ tsp	freshly ground black pepper

1. Bring plenty of salted water to a boil in a large saucepan.
2. Add sweet potato and cook until tender.
3. Drain potato and return to the saucepan.
4. Add Earth Balance, rice milk, sea salt, and pepper. Mash potato with a potato masher, incorporating other ingredients.
5. Serve right away or put the lid on the saucepan and set aside to keep warm.

Rich Mushroom Gravy

2 tbsp	sunflower oil
2 cups	sliced mushrooms
⅔ cup	finely diced onion
2	cloves garlic, minced
2 tbsp	nutritional yeast flakes
2 tsp	tamari
¼ tsp	freshly ground black pepper
pinch	dried rosemary
pinch	dried thyme
pinch	dried sage
¼ cup	spelt or gluten-free flour
2 ½ cups	vegetable stock
	sea salt

1. Heat oil in a saucepan over medium-high heat.
2. Add mushrooms, onion, and garlic and cook until browned, moving onion out of the way and pressing mushrooms to bottom of pan so they brown.
3. Add yeast, tamari, pepper, and herbs, stirring to mix.
4. Add flour and ¼ cup of the stock. Stir to combine and cook for 2 minutes to cook the flour.
5. Gradually add rest of stock, stirring constantly to prevent lumps.
6. Bring mixture to a boil, then reduce heat and simmer for 5 minutes. Taste and add salt to taste.
7. Serve right away or set aside and reheat when needed.

Pecan-Crusted Tempeh

1	block tempeh
1 cup	water
1 tsp	garlic powder
½ tsp	sea salt
4	bay leaves
2 tbsp or more	olive oil, for cooking

Paste

8 tbsp	flour of your choice
2 tbsp	Engevita (inactive) yeast
¼ tsp	sea salt
½ cup	unsweetened, unflavoured rice milk

Coating

1 cup	finely chopped pecans

1. Cut tempeh into 12 slices.
2. Combine water, garlic powder, sea salt, and bay leaves in a small bowl or measuring cup. Lay tempeh in a single layer in a shallow container. Cover with marinade and let sit in the fridge for at least 2 hours or, ideally, overnight.
3. When ready to cook the tempeh, drain off marinade and discard. Let tempeh sit on a plate to dry out a bit while you prepare the paste.
4. For paste, combine the flour, yeast, and sea salt in a shallow container. Add rice milk gradually, stirring with a fork to prevent lumps.
5. For coating, spread pecans into a shallow container or on a plate.
6. Dip a slice of tempeh into the paste, coating all sides. Place slice in pecans and coat all sides, pressing pecans onto the sides so they stick. Set each coated piece on a baking sheet. You can store them in the fridge at this point, or cook them right away.
7. If cooking the tempeh in the oven, drizzle each slice with about ¼ tsp olive oil, and put into a 400°F oven. Cook for 7 minutes, remove from oven, turn over, and drizzle other side with another ¼ tsp or so olive oil. Return to oven for 7 to 10 minutes or until nicely browned and crispy.
8. If cooking tempeh on the stovetop, heat olive oil in a frying pan over medium-high heat. Add slices and cook, flipping to brown both sides, until heated through and crispy.

Roasted Portobellos

4	large Portobello mushrooms
3 to 6 tsp	olive oil
2 to 4 tsp	tamari

1. Remove and discard mushroom stems. Wash mushroom caps under running water.
2. Drizzle top of mushrooms with olive oil, rubbing it in to coat the entire surface, to prevent drying out in the oven.
3. Place mushrooms on a baking sheet, gill-side up, and drizzle with olive oil and tamari to taste. Bake in a 400°F oven for about 10 minutes or until tender.

Sauces + Dressings

Amba

This sweet and slightly spicy sauce is one of the three sauces on the Middle Eastern Platter (page 16). It will keep for a couple of weeks in the fridge. You'll find fenugreek at Indian groceries. The little yellow granules give a pungent and unusual flavour to this sauce. Fenugreek has a certain bitterness, but when cooked, it adds a complexity of flavour—it is actually used in making imitation maple flavouring because of its caramel-like taste.

Makes about 1 cup

4 tsp	sunflower oil
½ tsp	mustard seeds
1 tsp	fenugreek seeds, ground
1 cup	finely chopped mango
1 tsp	Mexican chili powder
½ tsp	crushed dried chilies
1 cup	water
½ cup	organic sugar
¼ tsp	sea salt

1. Heat oil in a pot over medium-high heat. Add mustard seeds. As soon as they start to pop, add fenugreek. Stir and reduce heat to low so the seeds don't pop out of the pot. Let cook a few seconds.
2. Add mango, chili powder, and chilies and stir.
3. Pour in water, increase heat to high, bring to a boil, partially cover pot, and let mango steam for 2 or 3 minutes.
4. Add sugar and sea salt, bring mixture to a boil, reduce heat, and let simmer for 10 minutes.
5. Remove from heat.
6. Let cool before refrigerating.

Avocado Chipotle Sauce

Use this sauce on the Black Bean Tostada (page 14) or in the 7 Layer Dip (page 12). If you are making it for the 7 Layer Dip, use a food processor instead of a blender and add only the very minimum amount of water needed to keep the processor going, as you want it to be quite thick for the dip.

Makes about 2 cups

½ cup	water
½ cup	chopped cilantro
2 tbsp	lemon juice
1 tbsp	lime juice
1 tbsp	minced chipotle pepper or ¼ tsp chipotle powder
¼ to ½ tsp	sea salt
1	clove garlic or 1 tsp garlic powder
1 ½ cups	chopped avocado (about 2 medium avocadoes)

1. Purée water, cilantro, lemon and lime juice, chipotle, ¼ tsp sea salt, and garlic in a blender until liquefied.
2. Add avocado and blend.
3. Taste and add remaining ¼ tsp sea salt if needed.

Beach Sauce

This sauce is great to have in the fridge, ready to put on rice or noodles for a quick Fresh bowl. Just top with veggies and beans and you have an instant healthy meal.

Makes 1 cup

¾ cup	olive oil
¼ cup	tamari
1 ½ tsp	Mixed Herbs (page 131)

1. Put all ingredients in a bottle or bowl and mix well to combine.

Creamy Herb Dressing

You can adjust the herbs in this dressing to suit your taste buds or to suit what you have growing on your windowsill. It may seem strange to have to cook some vegetables to make a salad dressing, but that's what helps to make the tofu less tofu-ish. Tofu has a bad reputation because many people eat it plain, expecting it to taste good that way. But you wouldn't hand someone an onion and expect them to enjoy it—you have to do something to it, or use it as just one ingredient of many. Think of tofu in the same way.

Makes about 2 cups, or enough for 6 servings

2 tsp	sunflower oil
½ cup	chopped onion
½ cup	chopped carrot
¼ cup	chopped celery
3	cloves garlic, sliced
¼ tsp	sea salt
1 cup	vegetable stock
3 tbsp	water
2 tsp	apple cider vinegar or lemon juice
1 tsp	Dijon mustard
¼ cup	sunflower oil
1 cup	silken tofu
½ tsp	sea salt
1 tsp	freshly ground black pepper
1 cup	mixed fresh herbs (e.g., cilantro, parsley, chives, dill, oregano, mint)
¼ cup	chopped green onion

1. Heat 2 tsp sunflower oil in a frying pan over medium-low heat. Add onion, carrot, celery, garlic, and sea salt. Cook, stirring often, until vegetables are softened but not browned.
2. Add stock and simmer until carrots are tender and most of the liquid has evaporated.
3. Remove from heat and let cool (to speed this up, transfer the mixture to a bowl and put it in the fridge).
4. Once carrot mixture is cool, put the ingredients in a blender in the following order: water, vinegar, mustard, ¼ cup sunflower oil, tofu, sea salt, pepper, carrot mixture, herbs and green onion. You need the liquid to be down by the blades so that it won't clog up.
5. Blend until smooth.
6. Refrigerate until ready to use. If the dressing is too thick, add a bit of water or stock.

Caesar Dressing

This dressing has been serving us well for over 10 years now. Try it on the Chopped Caesar (page 46). Traditionally, white pepper is always used in light-coloured sauces so that there won't be visible black flecks in the sauce, but if you don't have white pepper, go ahead and use freshly ground black pepper.

Makes about 2 cups

2	cloves garlic, minced
¾ cup	silken tofu
½ cup	olive oil
¼ cup	water
2 tbsp	lemon juice
1 tbsp	apple cider vinegar
4 tsp	capers
2 ½ tsp	Dijon mustard
¾ tsp	ground white pepper
½ tsp	sea salt

1. Combine all ingredients in a blender.
2. Process until smooth, scraping down the sides of the processor bowl as needed.

House Dressing

This dressing is the favourite of all of our staff, that's why it is now our house dressing. It keeps for a week or more in the fridge. If you don't have flax oil, you can use all sunflower or add any other tasty oil, like avocado, hemp, or pumpkin seed.

Makes about 1½ cups

¼ cup	water
¼ cup	apple cider vinegar
2 tsp	sea salt
1 tsp	lemon juice
¾ tsp	freshly ground black pepper
¾ tsp	tamari
¼ tsp	organic sugar
¼ tsp	mustard powder
1	clove garlic
¾ cup	sunflower oil
¼ cup	flax oil

1. In a blender, purée all ingredients except sunflower and flax oils.
2. With blender running, add oils in a thin stream until dressing is emulsified.

Peanut Lime Dressing

This dressing will keep for up to a week in the fridge. It is delicious on the Tangled Thai Salad (page 61) but would be equally good on any salad or even poured on top of cold noodles.

Makes 1 cup

3	cloves garlic, minced (about 1 tbsp)
2 tbsp	tightly packed cilantro
2 tbsp	natural peanut butter
2 tbsp	
+ 2 tsp	lime juice
1 tbsp	
+ ½ tsp	tamari
1 tbsp	rice vinegar
1 tbsp	peeled and chopped ginger
2 tsp	coconut milk
1 ½ tsp	organic sugar
¾ tsp	sesame oil
¾ tsp	sambal oelek
½ cup	sunflower oil

1. In a blender, purée all ingredients except sunflower oil.

2. With blender running, add sunflower oil in a thin stream until dressing is emulsified.

Poppy Seed Dressing

This dressing should be quite thick. The trick to this is to add the oil very slowly at first to achieve an emulsification. Don't be tempted to pour it in too fast or the dressing will end up thin and will also separate. Just take your time—it will be worth it. It will last for a few days in the fridge.

Makes 1 cup

⅓ cup	apple cider vinegar
¾ cup	organic sugar
2 tbsp	chopped onion
1 tsp	dry mustard
1 tsp	sea salt
1 cup	sunflower oil
4 tsp	poppy seeds

1. In a blender, purée vinegar, sugar, onion, mustard, and sea salt.

2. With the blender running, very slowly add the oil. Start out with just drops, then gradually increase to a thin stream.

3. Pour dressing into a bowl and stir in poppy seeds.

Fresh Mayo

We've been making this mayo for over a decade now, and I still love it. It keeps in the fridge for about 3 or 4 days.

Makes about 1 cup

½	onion, diced
1 clove	garlic, minced
4 tbsp	vegetable stock or water
2 tsp	white wine
¼ tsp	Mixed Herbs (page 131)
pinch	sea salt
pinch	nutmeg
pinch	freshly ground black pepper
1 cup	silken tofu
3 tbsp	sunflower oil
1 tbsp	organic sugar
2 tsp	apple cider vinegar
2 tsp	miso
2 tsp	Dijon mustard

1. Mix together onion, garlic, stock, wine, herbs, sea salt, nutmeg, and pepper in a frying pan and cook over medium heat until liquid has evaporated.

2. Remove from heat and allow to cool.

3. In a blender, process onion mixture, tofu, oil, sugar, vinegar, miso, and mustard until smooth. Add water as needed for desired consistency.

Green Dressing

This bright green dressing keeps for up to a week in the fridge. The wasabi adds a little kick to the sweet herbal flavour.

1 ¼ cups	chopped cilantro
¼ cup	rice vinegar
¼ cup	water
2	cloves garlic, minced
2 tsp	peeled and chopped ginger
2 tbsp	sunflower oil
2 tbsp	agave nectar
¼ tsp	wasabi

1. In a blender, purée cilantro, vinegar, water, garlic, and ginger.

2. Add oil, agave nectar, and wasabi and blend until smooth.

Pesto

Our pesto recipe proves that you don't need parmesan to make a rich and decadent pesto. It keeps for a couple of weeks in the fridge and also freezes very well, but it's at its best and creamiest when freshly made.

Makes 1 cup

2	large cloves garlic
6 tbsp	raw sunflower seeds
⅓ cup	raw pine nuts
½ to ¾ tsp	sea salt
1 cup	tightly packed baby spinach
1 ½ cups	tightly packed fresh basil, large stems removed
½ cup	olive oil

1. Process garlic in a food processor until minced.
2. Add sunflower seeds, pine nuts, and ½ tsp salt and process until finely chopped.
3. Add spinach and process until finely chopped.
4. Add half of the basil and half of the olive oil. Process until mixed.
5. Add remaining basil and oil and process, scraping down sides with a spatula a couple of times.
6. Taste and add remaining ¼ tsp salt if needed.

Red Pesto

Sun-dried tomatoes come in various forms; you'll need ready-to-eat ones for this recipe. If yours came in a bag and are really dry, bring a pot of water to a boil, drop the tomatoes in, and leave for a few minutes to rehydrate. If yours are in a jar packed in oil, you can use the oil they were packed in instead of the olive oil from the recipe. Or try to find the type we use at the restaurants, which are vacuum-packed. They're nice and soft, and ready to go.

Makes ½ cup

1	small clove garlic
¼ cup	fresh basil
2 tbsp	raw sunflower seeds
2 tbsp	fresh tarragon
¼ tsp	sea salt
⅛ tsp	crushed dried chilies or sambal oelek
¼ cup	sun-dried tomatoes
1 ½ tsp	lemon juice
¼ cup	olive oil

1. In a food processor, process garlic, basil, sunflower seeds, tarragon, sea salt, and chilies until finely chopped. Scrape down sides of processor bowl with a spatula once or twice.
2. Add sun-dried tomatoes and lemon juice. Process until tomatoes are finely chopped.
3. With processor running, add olive oil and process, scraping sides down with a spatula a couple of times, until all ingredients are incorporated.

Salsa

This salsa is so flavourful and quick to make that you might never buy a jar of salsa again!

Makes about 2 cups

½ cup	tightly packed cilantro
¼ cup	chopped onion
¼ cup	pickled jalapeño peppers
1 ½ cups	canned tomatoes
⅛ tsp	sea salt
⅛ tsp	organic sugar

1. Pulse cilantro, onion, and jalapeños in a food processor for 2 or 3 seconds, just long enough to cut them up.
2. Add tomatoes, sea salt, and sugar. Process until mixed but still chunky.

Tahini Sauce

This versatile sauce can be used in several ways: as a dip for falafel, as a sauce on rice or soba noodles, or as a salad dressing. It will keep for up to 4 days in the fridge.

Makes 1 cup

2	cloves garlic, minced
½ cup	chopped parsley
2 tbsp	lemon juice
½ tsp	sea salt
⅔ cup	water
½ cup	tahini

1. In a blender, process garlic, parsley, lemon juice, and sea salt until smooth.
2. Add water and tahini. Blend until smooth.

Zhug

This easy-to-make hot sauce lasts for weeks in the fridge and brings a bright green spiciness to any of your favourite dishes. It is one of the trio of sauces on the Middle Eastern Platter (page 16).

Makes 1 cup

12	serrano chilies, stems removed and discarded, coarsely chopped
1	head garlic, peeled (10 to 12 cloves)
1 cup	tightly packed cilantro, thick stems removed
¼ tsp	ground cumin
¼ tsp	sea salt
	olive or sunflower oil

1. Put all ingredients except oil in a food processor and chop finely, scraping down the sides with a spatula a couple of times.
2. Pour sauce into a jar, then pour oil over the top to just cover.
3. Cover jar and refrigerate.

Brunch + Sweets

Breakfast Wraps

At Fresh we have a rotating roster of brunch burritos, all with the common element of scrambled tofu. We use 12-inch whole-wheat tortillas, but these recipes are for 8-inch tortillas, which are more readily available. We heat the tortillas on a grill, but at home you can use a toaster, a frying pan, the microwave, or oven. These three wraps are the most popular for brunch at Fresh these days. We offer them with an option of adding vegan or real cheese, and with soup, salad, or fries on the side. For a quick breakfast on the go, the wrap alone is enough, but for a bigger meal, serve it with a side.

Each recipe makes 4 wraps

Brunch Burrito

2 tbsp	canola oil
8	uncooked slices Tempeh Bacon (page 127)
8	thick slices tomato
pinch	sea salt
pinch	freshly ground black pepper
4	8-inch whole-wheat tortillas
8 tsp	mayonnaise of your choice
1	batch Scrambled Tofu (page 121)
2 cups	salad greens of your choice
1 cup	alfalfa sprouts

1. Heat oil in a frying pan over medium-high heat. Add tempeh slices and cook, flipping to brown on both sides, until heated through and crispy. Transfer to a paper towel to absorb any excess oil.
2. Add a splash of oil if needed to the pan, then add tomato slices. Sprinkle with sea salt and pepper. Cook tomatoes on both sides until browned and slightly softened.
3. Heat tortillas, then spread each with 2 tsp mayonnaise.
4. Divide Scrambled Tofu, salad greens, tomato slices, tempeh slices, and alfalfa sprouts among tortillas.
5. Fold edges in and roll up. Cut in half on the diagonal.

Bacon Mushroom Wrap

4 tsp	canola oil
8	slices uncooked Tempeh Bacon (page 127)
4 cups	sliced mushrooms
4	8-inch whole-wheat tortillas
8 tsp	mayonnaise of your choice
1	batch Scrambled Tofu (page 121)
1 cup	chopped tomatoes
pinch	sea salt
pinch	freshly ground black pepper
4 cups	salad greens of your choice

1. Heat canola oil in a frying pan over medium-high heat. Add tempeh slices and cook, flipping to brown on both sides, until cooked through and crispy. Transfer to a paper towel to absorb any excess oil.
2. Add a splash of oil if needed to the pan, and add mushrooms. Cook until browned on both sides.
3. Heat tortillas, then spread each with 2 tsp mayonnaise.
4. Top each tortilla with Scrambled Tofu, tempeh slices, mushrooms, and tomatoes. Sprinkle with sea salt and pepper.
5. Divide salad greens among tortillas.
6. Fold edges in and roll up. Cut in half on the diagonal.

Avocado Breakfast Wrap

4	8-inch whole-wheat tortillas
8 tsp	mayonnaise of your choice
1	batch Scrambled Tofu (page 121)
1	avocado, cut into 12 slices
24	grape tomatoes, halved
pinch	sea salt
pinch	freshly ground black pepper
2 cups	salad greens of your choice
¼ to ½ cup	chopped cilantro

1. Heat tortillas, then spread each with 2 tsp mayonnaise.
2. Top each tortilla with ½ cup Scrambled Tofu, then avocado slices and tomato halves.
3. Sprinkle with salt and pepper.
4. Divide salad greens and cilantro among tortillas.
5. Fold edges in and roll up. Cut in half on the diagonal.

Chocolate Babka

This recipe comes to us from Ilana Kadonoff, owner of Sweets from the Earth, the fabulous vegan bakery that makes all of our desserts. This is a favourite recipe of Ilana's and now a favourite of mine. I'm reminded of Jerry and Elaine fighting over the babka in that *Seinfeld* episode when I eat this one. Have it for breakfast or as an afternoon snack.

Ilana says you can make the whole thing and let it rise overnight in the fridge, covered, then bake it fresh in the morning. Let it come to room temperature before baking.

**Makes 2 standard loaves
(8 ½ x 4 ½ x 2 ½ inches)**

Dough

¾ cup	non-dairy milk, warmed to 110°F (warm, not hot, to the touch)
2 tsp	organic sugar
1 tbsp	dry active yeast
½ cup	puréed silken tofu
½ cup	sunflower oil (or other neutral-tasting vegetable oil)
	seeds of 1 vanilla bean or 1 tsp pure vanilla extract
3 cups	all-purpose wheat or spelt flour
¾ tsp	sea salt

Filling

¼ cup	sunflower oil, plus extra for brushing
¼ cup	organic sugar
1 cup	finely chopped dark chocolate
	non-dairy milk, for brushing

1. In a mixing bowl or the bowl of an electric stand mixer, combine warm milk and sugar. Sprinkle yeast on top. Set aside in a draft-free area for about 10 minutes, until mixture becomes foamy. Stir. (If mixture does not foam, the milk may have been too cold or hot. Discard and start again.)

2. Combine tofu, ½ cup oil, and vanilla bean seeds. Stir into yeast mixture and mix to incorporate.

3. Combine flour and sea salt, then mix gradually into the wet mixture. If using an electric mixer, use the dough hook and mix for 3 to 4 minutes. If mixing by hand, stir with a wooden spoon. Mixture will be thick. Once dough comes together, transfer to a floured surface and knead gently by hand a few times to form a ball. *Do not* knead until smooth. Dough should remain slightly sticky. Transfer to a lightly oiled bowl, cover with a damp cloth, and let rise in a warm, draft-free spot for about an hour.

4. Once dough has doubled in bulk, punch down and transfer to a floured surface. Divide into two pieces. Roll out 1 piece to a 10- × 18-inch rectangle.

5. To add the filling, using a pastry brush, brush 2 tbsp of the oil onto dough. Sprinkle with half of the sugar and half of the chocolate.

6. Roll dough into a log, pinching seams at end. Form log into a ring, pinching ends together. Lift gently and twist the ring, tucking ends underneath. Place the twist into a lightly oiled 8 ½- × 4 ½- × 2 ½-inch loaf pan.

7. Roll out remaining dough and repeat Steps 5 and 6.

8. Cover loaf pans with lightly oiled plastic wrap (oil side toward dough) and let sit until it has doubled in size (about 1 ½ hours).

9. Preheat oven to 350°F.

10. Brush tops of loaves with milk. Bake for about 40 minutes, until tops are golden brown and tester inserted into the centre comes out clean. Turn out from pans and let cool on a wire rack or enjoy warm.

Granola Parfaits

Every weekend at the restaurants, we make a different fruit compote to go with our granola parfaits. Here are six versions. You can use either fresh or frozen berries, or a mixture of both. If you're using fresh strawberries, just remove the stems and cut them in half. If using frozen, you can use them whole. You can use whichever kind of apples you like, but I am partial to Granny Smith or McIntosh. To make the parfaits, layer equal amounts of Decadent Granola (page 120), yogurt of your choice (soy if you like), and one of these compotes in a sundae dish.

If you have time, make a really rich parfait by draining fat-free dairy yogurt (this works only with dairy yogurt, not soy) in a coffee filter set in a strainer over a bowl. Refrigerate for a few hours until most of the liquid has drained out. You'll be left with thick, rich yogurt with no fat.

Each recipe makes about 3 cups

Raspberry and Apple with Goji Berries Compote

3 cups	raspberries
¼ cup	agave nectar
1 tbsp	goji berries
¼ tsp	pure vanilla extract
1 tbsp	water
1 tbsp	cornstarch
1 cup	peeled, cored, and sliced apples

1. Mix together raspberries, agave nectar, goji berries, and vanilla in a saucepan.
2. Bring mixture to a boil over medium-high heat.
3. Cook for 5 to 10 minutes, until fruits are very soft.
4. Combine water and cornstarch and add to saucepan.
5. Stir, bring mixture to a boil, then remove from heat.
6. Stir in sliced apples and let cool.

Pineapple, Raspberry, and Ginger Compote

1 ½ cups	chopped pineapple
1 ½ cups	raspberries
2	thick slices ginger (each about 3 inches long)
¼ cup	agave nectar
1 tbsp	water
1 tbsp	cornstarch

1. Mix together pineapple, raspberries, ginger, and agave nectar in a saucepan.
2. Bring mixture to a boil over medium-high heat.
3. Cook for 5 to 10 minutes, until fruits are very soft.
4. Combine water and cornstarch and add to saucepan.
5. Stir, bring mixture to a boil, then remove from heat.
6. Remove and discard ginger.
7. Allow to cool.

Blueberry and Apple with Cinnamon Compote

1 ½ cups	peeled, cored, and sliced apples
1 ½ cups	blueberries
¼ cup	agave nectar
⅛ tsp	ground cinnamon
pinch	nutmeg
1 tbsp	water
1 tbsp	cornstarch

1. Mix together apples, blueberries, agave nectar, cinnamon, and nutmeg in a saucepan.
2. Bring mixture to a boil over medium-high heat.
3. Cook for 5 to 10 minutes, until fruits are very soft.
4. Combine water and cornstarch and add to saucepan.
5. Stir, bring mixture to a boil, then remove from heat.
6. Allow to cool.

Strawberry and Pineapple with Raisins Compote

1 ½ cups	strawberries
1 ½ cups	chopped pineapple
¼ cup	agave nectar
2 tbsp	raisins
1 tbsp	water
1 tbsp	cornstarch

1. Mix together strawberries, pineapple, agave nectar, and raisins in a saucepan.
2. Bring mixture to a boil over medium-high heat.
3. Cook for 5 to 10 minutes, until fruits are very soft.
4. Combine water and cornstarch and add to saucepan.
5. Stir, bring mixture to a boil, then remove from heat.
6. Allow to cool.

Triple Berry Compote

1 cup	strawberries
1 cup	raspberries
1 cup	blueberries
¼ cup	agave nectar
1 tbsp	water
1 tbsp	cornstarch
1 cup	peeled, cored, and sliced apples

1. Mix berries with agave nectar in a saucepan.
2. Bring mixture to a boil over medium-high heat.
3. Cook for 5 to 10 minutes, until fruits are very soft.
4. Combine water and cornstarch and add to saucepan.
5. Stir, bring mixture to a boil, then remove from heat.
6. Stir in sliced apples and let cool.

Strawberry and Mango with Goji Berries Compote

1 ½ cups	strawberries
1 ½ cups	chopped mango
¼ cup	agave nectar
1 tbsp	goji berries
¼ tsp	pure vanilla extract
1 tbsp	water
1 tbsp	cornstarch

1. Mix together strawberries, mango, agave nectar, goji berries, and vanilla in a saucepan.
2. Bring mixture to a boil over medium-high heat.
3. Cook for 5 to 10 minutes, until fruits are very soft.
4. Combine water and cornstarch and add to saucepan.
5. Stir, bring mixture to a boil, then remove from heat.
6. Allow to cool.

Decadent Granola

I've been dreaming about a big, chunky, crispy granola, kind of like the Quaker Harvest Crunch I loved as a kid. I was trying to figure out how to achieve this for a while, and I finally found a method that gives great results. When I gave the granola to my friend Fiona to taste test, she said it was decadent, and I knew right then that that would be its name. Using whole nuts really pushes this into a different league from your average granola. This granola takes a while to make, but you can be doing other things while it's in the oven, since all you have to do is stir it a couple of times. The secret to the chunkiness is the quick-cook oats. Regular oats don't form the chunks. They still taste good, but it was the big chunks that I was going for. If you can't find the quinoa flakes, use all oats. Your oven timer will be your best friend when making this granola. If you've never used it before, you will today.

Makes about 6 cups

3 cups	quick-cook oats
1 cup	quick-cook quinoa flakes
½ cup	flaxseed meal
½ cup	whole raw pistachios
½ cup	raw pecan halves
¼ cup	whole raw cashews
¼ cup	chopped Brazil nuts
½ cup	unsweetened, unflavoured rice milk
½ cup	maple syrup
½ cup	organic sugar
¼ cup	canola oil
¼ cup	coconut oil
½ tsp	pure vanilla extract
¼ tsp	sea salt
½ cup	raisins (optional)
½ cup	sliced dried apricots (optional)

1. Preheat oven to 325°F.
2. Mix together oats, quinoa flakes, flaxseed meal, and nuts in a large bowl.
3. In a small pot over medium-low heat, combine rice milk, maple syrup, sugar, oils, vanilla, and sea salt. Stir frequently until sugar is dissolved and coconut oil is melted.
4. Pour liquid mixture over dry mixture, stirring to coat.
5. Spread oat mixture on a large baking sheet and bake in oven for 30 minutes.
6. Remove tray from oven and reduce oven temperature to 225°F (leaving the door open for a minute will help it cool).
7. Stir granola and return to oven for 10 minutes.
8. Remove tray from oven, stir granola again, and return to oven for another 10 minutes.
9. Turn off the oven, set the timer for 1 hour, leaving the granola in the oven. After 1 hour, remove from oven, add raisins and apricots, and let cool.
10. Store in an airtight container or zip-lock bag.

Scrambled Tofu

This recipe is the cornerstone of many of our brunch specials, such as the Avocado Breakfast Wrap (page 115), Brunch Burrito (page 114), Bacon Mushroom Wrap (page 115), and Tex-Mex Tortilla Scramble (page 122).

Makes 2 cups

2 tbsp	olive oil
1	onion, finely diced
1	clove garlic, minced
1 tbsp	Engevita (inactive) yeast
1 tsp	garlic powder
¾ tsp	dried dill
½ tsp	sea salt
½ tsp	freshly ground black pepper
pinch	turmeric
¼ cup	water
2 cups	chopped firm tofu

1. Heat oil in a frying pan over medium-high heat.
2. Add onion and garlic and cook until softened, stirring often.
3. In a small bowl, mix together yeast, garlic powder, dill, sea salt, pepper, and turmeric. Add water and stir to make a paste.
4. Crumble tofu into very small pieces and add to pan.
5. Pour in paste, stirring to mix thoroughly.
6. Bring mixture to a boil, stirring until heated through and liquid has evaporated.

Instant Turtles

Whenever I can persuade someone to sit downstairs and keep me company in the basement at Fresh on Bloor while I do the weekly inventory, I ply them with what I call instant turtles. I always loved Turtles chocolates—that combo of pecans, chocolate, and caramel is so good!—and I like to think of dates as nature's caramel, so this combination really works to give you that familiar Turtles taste. I know this is more of a concept than an actual recipe, but I wanted to share it with you, since it's such an easy treat and really hits the spot when you're having a candy craving.

Makes 1 turtle

1	date
2	pecan halves
6	mini vegan chocolate chips

1. Put them all in your mouth together and enjoy!

Tex-Mex Tortilla Scramble

This is one of our most popular brunch specials. It has a bit of spice to really get your day started. If you want it even spicier, add a splash of your favourite hot sauce. You can add vegan or dairy cheese to this as well. When cooking the tortillas, brush them with oil for a real golden-brown look. If you don't want to use oil, they will still be crispy, just not as brown.

Serves 4

8	6-inch sprouted corn tortillas
2 tsp	canola oil (optional)
	sea salt
1 cup	chopped salad greens of your choice
1	batch Scrambled Tofu (page 121)
1	batch Avocado Chipotle Sauce (page 103)
1 cup	chopped tomato
¼ to ½ cup	chopped cilantro
2 cups	cooked brown rice
1	batch Black Bean Mix (page 130)
1	avocado, cut into 12 slices
¼ cup	chopped green onions

1. Preheat oven to 400°F.
2. Place corn tortillas on a baking sheet and brush each with ¼ tsp canola oil (⅛ tsp per side). Bake until crispy, remove from oven and sprinkle with sea salt.
3. On each of 4 plates, arrange ¼ cup salad greens. Place 2 tortillas on top of the greens, slightly overlapping each other.
4. Spread ½ cup Scrambled Tofu down the centre of each tortilla. Top with one-quarter of the Avocado Chipotle Sauce.
5. Scatter tomato and cilantro over tofu and sauce.
6. Scoop ½ cup each rice and Black Bean Mix onto each plate, beside tortillas.
7. Top with avocado slices and green onions.

Lemon Blueberry Pancakes

The easiest way to get an intense lemon presence in a recipe without the sourness is to use lemon zest or lemon flavouring from a bottle. In this recipe, I didn't want the texture of lemon zest, so I used organic lemon flavouring. You can find it at better grocery stores. Just make sure that the only ingredients are lemon and oil. If you have leftovers of this pancake batter, you will need to add a bit more rice milk before cooking it, as it will thicken as it sits.

Serves 4 to 6

4 cups	Bob's Red Mill GF All Purpose Baking Flour
½ cup	flaxseed meal
2 ½ tsp	baking powder
2 tsp	baking soda
½ tsp	sea salt
2 cups	vanilla-flavoured rice milk
½ cup	agave nectar
4 tsp	organic lemon flavour
	sunflower or canola oil, for cooking
1 cup	fresh blueberries

1. Mix together flour, flaxseed, baking powder and soda, and sea salt in a large bowl.
2. Mix rice milk with agave nectar and lemon flavour in a small bowl or measuring cup. It's okay if the agave nectar doesn't mix well with the rice milk.
3. Make a well in the centre of the dry ingredients. Pour a little of the liquid into the well and stir with a wooden spoon. Gradually add more liquid, stirring each time and incorporating more and more of the dry ingredients from the sides of the well, until all the liquid is incorporated.
4. Heat oil in a frying pan over medium heat. Using a small ladle or spoon, scoop batter into pan. Drop fresh blueberries on top of each pancake, enough so there will be a blueberry in every bite.
5. When pancakes are browned on the bottom sides, flip over and cook until other sides are browned and pancakes are cooked through.
6. Repeat Steps 4 and 5 with remaining batter, lightly oiling the pan again if needed.
7. Serve immediately, blueberry-side up, with maple syrup and Earth Balance or butter.

Pineapple Flax Pancakes

These gluten-free pancakes are so easy to make, you don't have to save them for the weekends only. If you don't want to buy a whole pineapple, look for precut or canned chunks and slice them a couple of milli-metres thick. This recipe calls for gluten-free flour, but you can easily substitute any flour that you like to use. We use Bob's Red Mill GF (Gluten Free) All Purpose Baking Flour, available at health food stores and many grocery stores. If you used a can of pineapple and you're feeling ambitious, make the Pineapple Syrup, and if not, serve with maple syrup and Earth Balance or butter.

Serves 4 to 6

4 cups	Bob's Red Mill GF All Purpose Baking Flour
½ cup	flaxseed meal
2 ½ tsp	baking powder
2 tsp	baking soda
½ tsp	sea salt
2 cups	vanilla-flavoured rice milk
½ cup	agave nectar
1 cup	finely sliced pineapple
	sunflower or canola oil, for cooking

1. Mix together flour, flaxseed, baking powder and soda, and sea salt in a large bowl.
2. Mix rice milk with agave nectar in a small bowl or measuring cup. It's okay if the agave nectar doesn't mix well with the rice milk.
3. Make a well in the centre of the dry ingredients. Pour a little of the liquid into the well and stir with a wooden spoon. Gradually add more li-quid, stirring each time and incorporating more and more of the dry ingredients from the sides of the well, until all the liquid is incorporated.
4. Heat oil in a frying pan over medium heat. Using a small ladle or spoon, scoop batter and place pineapple slices on top of each pancake, enough so there will be pineapple in every bite.

5. When pancakes are browned on the bottom sides, flip them over and cook until other sides are browned and pancakes are cooked through.
6. Repeat Steps 4 and 5 with remaining batter, lightly oiling the pan again if needed.
7. Serve immediately, pineapple-side up, with maple syrup and Earth Balance or butter.

Pineapple Syrup
To make pineapple syrup, pour the juice from the canned pineapple (about ⅔ cup) into a saucepan set over high heat. Boil liquid until reduced by half. (If you're not sure if it has reduced enough, pour it into a glass measuring cup to check.) Add an equal amount (about ⅓ cup) maple syrup, stirring to combine. Serve hot or cold.

Morning Glory

This recipe makes 4 to 5 cups of porridge. A full cup with the fruit on top makes a very filling breakfast, so you could easily get away with only ½ cup for children or those with a small appetite. Try using kitchen scissors to cut the dates and apricots. It's much easier this way, since each piece will stick on a knife. We garnish this porridge with banana and kiwi, but you could use strawberries, blueberries, apple, or any other fresh fruit or berry you like.

Serves 4 to 6

½ cup	steel-cut oats
½ cup	quinoa
½ cup	pearl barley
4 to 6 cups	water
4	dried apricots, sliced
4	dates, chopped
2 tbsp	currants
¼ tsp	sea salt

Garnishes

2	bananas, sliced
2	kiwi fruit, peeled and chopped
4 to 6 tbsp	vanilla rice milk
4 to 6 tsp	maple syrup
4 to 6 tsp	raw pumpkin seeds

1. Mix together oats, quinoa, and barley in a medium pot. Rinse by filling pot with water, stirring grains around with your hand, and then draining the water through a fine mesh strainer. Repeat 4 or 5 times, until the water is almost clear.

2. Stir in 4 cups of the water, apricots, dates, currants, and sea salt.

3. Bring mixture to a boil, then reduce heat to low, cover, and simmer until all water is absorbed, stirring occasionally.

4. Once all the water is absorbed, taste it to see if the grains are done to your liking. If too firm, add another 1 cup water and cook until absorbed. If the grains are then still too firm, add the last 1 cup of water and cook until absorbed.

5. Transfer to bowls and top each with banana, kiwi, rice milk, maple syrup, and pumpkin seeds.

Tempeh Bacon

In trying to replicate the taste of bacon, I've realized it's all about the smoke flavour. Liquid smoke tastes kind of yucky to me, though, and it never quite marries with whatever you're putting it in. I like using smoked paprika to get a smoky flavour because it's much less harsh than liquid smoke, and it seems to become a part of whatever you put it with, instead of always just tasting like itself. Smoked paprika comes in both sweet and hot versions. For this recipe, use the sweet. If you happen to be a fan of liquid smoke, you can use 1 tsp instead of the paprika in this recipe. Cut the Tempeh Bacon into strips and use in the Tempeh BLT Sandwich (page 71) or chopped into slices for the Chopped Caesar (page 46) or Good Salad (page 53). Freeze any uncooked bacon you're not planning to use right away. The best way to do this is to lay it on a baking sheet lined with plastic wrap. Once it is frozen, put the slices into a zip-lock bag and put back in the freezer. By individually quick-freezing them, later, when you're ready to use them, you will be able to thaw exactly as many slices as you need.

Makes about 25 to 35 slices of bacon, depending on the size of the tempeh block

1 block tempeh

Marinade
2 tbsp	smoked paprika
2 tsp	garlic powder
¼ cup	tamari
¼ cup	apple cider vinegar
¼ cup	water
¼ cup	sunflower oil
¼ cup	maple syrup

To marinate tempeh:
1. Put smoked paprika and garlic powder in a measuring cup with a spout. Add tamari, gradually at first, stirring to prevent lumps. Stir in remaining marinade ingredients.
2. Slice tempeh as thin as you can.
3. Lay tempeh slices in a baking dish or shallow plastic container in single layers, covering each layer with marinade before adding another layer.
4. Let marinate for at least 2 hours, or up to a couple of days, in the refrigerator.

To serve:
1. Heat oil in a frying pan over medium-high heat (use just enough oil to cover bottom of pan). Add tempeh slices to the pan and cook, flipping to brown both sides, until heated through and crispy. (Or, to bake, preheat oven to 350°F, place tempeh on a baking sheet and bake until browned and starting to crisp, about 15 minutes.)
2. Transfer tempeh to a paper towel to absorb any excess oil.

Etc.

Black Bean Mix

Use this delicious stew in the 7 Layer Dip (page 12), Black Bean Tostada (page 14), and Tex-Mex Tortilla Scramble (page 122). You can leave the black beans whole for a stew-like consistency, or mash them with an immersion blender or potato masher for a more pâté-like result. If you are making the 7 Layer Dip, mash it to a smooth consistency.

Makes 3 cups

1 cup	diced onions
2 tbsp	sunflower oil
2 tsp	coriander seeds, ground
1 ¼ tsp	Mexican chili powder
1 ¼ tsp	garlic powder
1 ¼ tsp	dried oregano
1 tsp	sea salt
¼ tsp	cayenne pepper
3	cloves garlic, minced
1 cup	chopped fresh or canned tomatoes
½ cup	water
½ cup	chopped cilantro
3 tbsp	tomato paste
1 tsp	diced canned chipotle pepper with adobo sauce or ¼ tsp chipotle powder
1	can (15 oz/425 g) black beans, drained and rinsed (or 2 cups cooked black beans)

1. Sauté onions in oil until softened.
2. Add coriander, chili and garlic powders, oregano, sea salt, and pepper. Cook for 1 or 2 minutes, stirring often.
3. Add garlic, tomatoes, water, cilantro, tomato paste, and chipotle. Stir to incorporate, then bring to a boil.
4. Stir in black beans.
5. Bring mixture to a boil, reduce heat, and simmer for 5 minutes.

Grilled Tofu Steaks

Makes 8 steaks

1	block (9 oz/250 g) firm tofu
2 cups	water
½ cup	tamari
2 tbsp	ground coriander
4 tsp	garlic powder
2 tbsp	canola oil, if cooking in a pan

1. Cut the tofu into four slices, then cut those slices on the diagonal to form 8 triangular pieces.
2. Mix water with tamari, coriander, and garlic powder in a bowl. Pour over tofu.
3. Let marinate at least 1 hour and up to 8 hours or overnight, in the fridge.
4. To cook, either place directly on a hot grill and cook on both sides until they have grill marks, or pan-fry with canola oil over medium-high heat, flipping to brown on both sides.

Mixed Herbs

We use this herb mixture in some of our recipes, and to sprinkle on regular fries and also our Sweet Potato Fries (page 23).

Makes ¾ cup

2 tbsp	dried basil
2 tbsp	dried oregano
2 tbsp	dried marjoram
2 tbsp	dried dill
2 tbsp	dried sage
1 tbsp	dried rosemary
1 tbsp	dried tarragon

1. Mix together herbs in a small bowl. Store in a covered container or shaker bottle.

BBQ Tempeh

Use this tempeh in the BBQ Tempeh Sandwich (page 69) and BBQ Tempeh and Aged Cheddar Sandwich (page 70), or to top a salad. If you're not using the BBQ Tempeh right away, you can freeze it. The best way to do this is to lay it on a cookie sheet lined with plastic wrap and place it in the freezer uncovered. Once the tempeh is frozen, transfer the slices to a zip-lock bag to store in the freezer. By individually quick-freezing the slices, later, when you're ready to use them, you will be able to thaw just as many as you need.

1 block	tempeh

Sauce

2 tbsp	olive oil
½	onion, peeled and diced
1	clove garlic, minced
1 tsp	allspice
½ tsp	cayenne pepper
¼ cup	organic sugar
6 tbsp	apple cider vinegar
6 tbsp	water
6 tbsp	ketchup
4 tsp	Bragg Liquid Aminos or tamari
4 tsp	molasses
2 tsp	sesame oil

1. Heat the olive oil in a pan over medium heat.
2. Add the onion, garlic, allspice, and cayenne. Sauté a few minutes, until onion is softened.
3. Add the sugar, vinegar, water, ketchup, Bragg, molasses, and sesame oil.
4. Bring the mixture to a boil, then reduce heat and simmer for 15 minutes or until the sauce is slightly thickened.
5. Remove from heat.
6. Cut tempeh into 16 even slices by cutting the block in half, then each half in half again, then in half again, and then in half again. (It's very hard to cut even slices just by eyeballing it.)
7. Lay tempeh in a single layer in a baking dish or other shallow container. Cover with sauce. (You may need to create 2 layers, depending on the size of your dish.)
8. Cover the container and refrigerate for at least 1 hour, or up to 2 days.

Nutrient Boosters

Elevate the nutrition in your everyday meals with these delicious mixes. Make one or more and keep in the fridge in a shaker bottle, which you can find at most kitchen supply stores, ready to add to cereal, salads, soups, pastas—anything!

Loomi powder, which is an optional addition to the Kick Start, is powdered sun-dried lime. In Toronto, it is available at The Spice Trader.

Whole flaxseeds don't give you the nutrients they do when they're ground; they just pass through your body undigested. So either buy them ground (look for "flaxseed meal") or grind them yourself in a spice grinder. Don't grind the flax seeds right down to a powder, just pulse enough to break up the seeds. Once ground, they can go rancid quite quickly, so keep refrigerated or frozen.

If chopping the nuts for the Protein Boost in a food processor, roughly chop the Brazil nuts with a knife first, otherwise the other ingredients will be puréed before the Brazil nuts break up. To prepare the nuts by hand, use a paring knife and halve them, then, holding the two halves together, shave down the edges to get tiny pieces. You want the pieces to be about the same size as the sunflower seeds. It takes a while, but I find it kind of meditative and relaxing.

Omega Shake

³/₄ cup each:

chia seeds
flaxseed meal
hemp seeds
pumpkin seeds
sesame seeds
sunflower seeds

Fibre Boost

2 tbsp each:

flaxseed meal
pumpkin seeds
sunflower seeds
finely chopped almonds
finely chopped pistachios
finely chopped walnuts
quick-cook oats, toasted in a 350°F
    oven for 5 minutes

Protein Boost

2 tbsp each:

chia seeds
flaxseed meal
hemp seeds
pumpkin seeds
sesame seeds
sunflower seeds
finely chopped Brazil nuts
finely chopped cashews
finely chopped hazelnuts
finely chopped pistachios

Kick Start

2 tbsp each:

chia seeds
flaxseed meal
hemp seeds
pumpkin seeds
sesame seeds
sunflower seeds
plus
⅛ tsp cayenne pepper
½ tsp loomi powder (optional)

Sun-Blushed Tomatoes

I had these tomatoes a few years ago in England, and I've been waiting all this time for them to come to Canada, but to no avail. So I decided to make them myself. They are sometimes called semi sun-dried tomatoes and are basically halfway between a raw tomato and a fully sun-dried one. They are fantastic on salads, sandwiches, pastas, pizzas, or anywhere, really. Here are three versions: plain, garlic, and garlic and herb. They will keep well in the fridge for up to 1 week.

Plain Sun-Blushed Tomatoes

4	plum tomatoes
2 tsp	olive oil
¼ tsp	organic sugar
¼ tsp	sea salt
¼ tsp	freshly ground black pepper

1. Preheat oven to 300°F.
2. Cut tomatoes in half lengthwise. Scoop out seeds with a spoon and discard.
3. Lay tomatoes cut-side up on a baking sheet.
4. In a small bowl, combine olive oil, sugar, sea salt, and pepper.
5. Drizzle oil mixture over tomatoes.
6. Bake in oven for about 3 hours or until tomatoes are wrinkly and look semi-dried. You don't want them to be totally dried.
7. Remove from oven and let cool.

Variations

For Garlic Sun-Blushed Tomatoes, add ½ tsp minced garlic to oil mixture.

For Garlic Herb Sun-Blushed Tomatoes, add ½ tsp minced garlic and 1 tsp each finely minced fresh oregano and thyme to oil mixture.

Tofu Ricotta Fritters

Who would think you could turn tofu into something decadent? Well, this is how you do it. These fritters take a little while to make, but they are totally worth it. They are part of the Spicy Noodles with Greens and Tofu Ricotta Fritters (page 93), but would be equally at home on top of your favourite pasta dish or salad.

Serves 4 (12 fritters)

Fritters

2	cloves garlic
2 cups	chopped firm tofu
3 tbsp	olive oil
2 tbsp	lemon juice
1 tsp	miso
½ tsp	sea salt
¼ tsp	dried rosemary or ½ tsp fresh
2 tbsp	spelt flour
	canola oil, for frying

Paste

¾ cup	unsweetened, unflavoured rice milk or water
¾ cup	spelt flour

Coating

1 ½ cups	puffed quinoa
1 ½ tsp	garlic powder
1 ½ tsp	sea salt

1. For fritters, mince garlic in a food processor.
2. Add tofu, olive oil, lemon juice, miso, sea salt, and rosemary, and pulse until finely chopped but not puréed. Scrape down sides of processor with a spatula a couple of times.
3. Add flour and pulse a couple of times to just mix.
4. Form mixture into 12 patties, pressing each between your palms to make it hold together. Set on a baking sheet or plate and refrigerate while you prepare the paste and coating.
5. For paste, in a shallow bowl, combine rice milk and flour to make a smooth paste.
6. For coating, in a shallow bowl, mix puffed quinoa with garlic powder and sea salt.
7. Coat each fritter by placing it in the paste and using a fork to spread the paste over the top.
8. Transfer fritter to coating mixture, pressing quinoa onto all surfaces. Place coated fritter on a plate or baking sheet.
9. Repeat Steps 7 and 8 with remaining patties. Once all fritters are coated, refrigerate for at least 15 minutes and up to 8 hours or overnight to firm up.
10. When ready to cook them, heat canola oil over medium-high heat in a frying pan. Add patties and cook for a few minutes on each side until nicely browned and crispy. Or bake in a 350°F oven on a baking sheet for 20 minutes, turning over after 10 minutes

Fresh Juices, Smoothies + Cocktails

Healthy Is the New Sexy

This year I celebrated a major milestone in my life. Twenty years have passed since I founded Juice for Life (now Fresh), quit university, took my student loan, bought my first commercial juicer, and went mobile with my travelling juice bar. In 2010, I retired from the daily running of Fresh restaurants for a much-needed extended sabbatical. I am writing the final pages of this cookbook from my hammock on the beach in Puerto Escondido, Oaxaca, Mexico. Soon I will return home to spring in Toronto, refreshed and renewed, to release this cookbook and grow Fresh to five locations.

Twenty years ago, I was 25 and full of evangelistic good intentions for the planet and all creatures, big and small. During those early years, I explored improving my health through macrobiotic, raw-food, and vegan diets, juice fasting, and food allergy testing. Going vegan and eliminating the offending foods, allergies, and bad habits coincided with the emergence of a new me in glowing good health, with an energetic sense of well-being.

I discovered my "fountain of youth" in juicing, along with a balanced vegan diet that relied heavily on legumes, sprouts, nuts, seeds, whole grains, fresh fruits, vegetables, superfoods, and nutritional supplements. I followed the dietary principles of proper food-combining from the ground-breaking book *Fit for Life*, by Harvey and Marilyn Diamond, and diligently excluded all packaged, canned, and processed foods, sugar and refined sweeteners, fried foods, alcohol, coffee and caffeine, wheat, corn, yeast, and salt.

I maintained this regimen for the next 18 years. During those years, my mission was to provide vegetarians and vegans with a hip haven where, for a change, they were number one, not an afterthought.

Fast-forward to 2011 and we are writing our fourth cookbook, and running three award-winning, booming Fresh locations with two more soon on the way. We employ more than 200 incredibly dedicated young staff members. This is all wonderful, but I must confess one thing before we continue. Three years ago my 17-year run as a strict vegan came to an end.

So what happened? It all started with a fractured floating rib from playing sports. As I healed, it occurred to me that my rib had snapped all too easily—just like that. Feeling apprehensive, I made an appointment for a bone density test. Sure enough, I discovered that I had lost 20 percent of my bone mass somewhere along the way. At 80 percent of my optimum bone mass, and with a recent fracture, I was declared osteopenic. I was dumbfounded.

During all those years, it had never occurred to me to take calcium supplements or to consider my genetic predisposition to decreased bone density. I ate plenty of calcium-rich leafy greens, and I thought that was enough, but it wasn't. My diet, habits, and identity shifted dramatically as I focused on increasing the calcium in my diet by eating organic yogurt, dairy products, and a tin of sardines every day. I also traded in my yoga pass and chilled-out lifestyle for a high-impact routine at the gym, which included running and weightlifting. I cut out all calcium-inhibiting foods from my diet and searched out calcium-enriched foods and beverages. I started taking calcium and vitamin D supplements, and two years later a test revealed that I had reversed the bone loss, regained 15 percent of my bone mass, and was no longer considered osteopenic. I like to joke that I am a medical miracle, but I'm not. The truth is I zeroed in on those nutritional and lifestyle factors that would tip the balance in my favour and I diligently followed through on them.

Soon after, I stepped into the "over 40" world of fertility clinics, fertility doctors, and fertility drugs. I suppose I had always taken it for granted that when I was ready to have kids it would happen easily and naturally. My sister has six wonderful kids, and my brother has four. Now it was my turn. After three painful miscarriages, I found myself sitting in the fertility clinic, patiently waiting my turn. I underwent four IVF treatments that led me to see a number of doctors, acupuncturists, and holistic nutritionists along the way.

In my search for the magic formula that would allow me to carry a baby to term, I received differing advice from everyone around me. A growing consensus pointed to my vegan-vegetarian diet. High-quality sources of iron and protein became my main dietary focus to thicken my uterine lining. I switched to eating organic red meat, lamb, and fresh fish on the recommendation of my fertility doctors. During daily ultrasounds and blood tests, the animal products did seem to fortify my body at a time when I needed it the most. However, despite these radical efforts, in the end I wasn't able to carry to term (one of the great disappointments of my charmed life). I will never know for certain what role my vegan diet played in my fertility challenges but I have certainly been humbled by the health challenges I have faced over the past five years.

I am the ultimate Fresh customer, always searching, adjusting, and changing in response to life's challenges and my body's demands for optimum health. I am an organic, all-natural vegetarian hippie, a vegan with an omnivore's worldview, a 100-miler, an "eat right for your blood type" devotee, a raw foodist, a fruitarian, a macrobiotic fanatic, a follower of Ayurvedic medicine, a gourmet-foodie, and a lover of this beautiful planet. What I love about Fresh is that I continue to find everything I need on our menus as I grow and change.

Possessing an abundance of fresh food and juice inspirations led Jennifer and me to the realization that it was time to write a new cookbook. This collection of vegetarian recipes reflects our evolution since *refresh*, our last cookbook, was published. Stretching our creativity, challenging ourselves, and pushing the Fresh envelope just a little farther. You will find that our personal experiences are woven into the very fabric of our creations and we invite you to join us on this fun exciting journey with us.

It is much more mainstream to be a vegetarian now compared with twenty years ago, when my vegan roots were on the fringe and alternative. People in general are better educated, more aware, and more accepting of healthy eating as a modern way of life. Being embarrassed or mocked about it are things of the past. My oft-repeated defence to challenge the stereotype that vegetarian food is bland or boring is no longer necessary.

Today, most inspired restaurateurs or talented chefs devote the same flair, creativity, and taste to their plant-based dishes as to the rest of their menus. Customers at the Fresh restaurants have also kept us on our toes, demanding our ingenuity with the dishes and juice we serve while simultaneously insisting that favourites remain staples on our menus. There would be a riot if we removed the Quinoa Onion Rings (page 19) for instance, the recipe for which you will find revealed here in this cookbook.

I believe there has never been a better time to be a vegan or vegetarian!

Living and loving life,
Ruth

Juicing

With juice bars popping up all over the place it might be tempting to think that juicing is a new trend. But it's really just the latest manifestation of a centuries-old practice. And in this new age of genetically modified, over-refined, chemical-laden foods, the rediscovery and rising popularity of juicing has never been more timely.

Jumping on the bandwagon, the celebrity-driven media has helped our industry immensely by highlighting our pop-culture role models, shiny and glowing, imbibing fresh juices, smoothies, and shakes made with the latest "hot" and trendy ingredients. The truth is that many of these celebrities who are in the business of looking good and defying the aging process really do stay ahead of the game by eating and drinking a mostly organic, plant-based diet. I know because when they are in Toronto, they come to us in their baseball caps, undercover, every day if they can. This past year we have seen everyone from the Jonas Brothers to Russell Brand tweet about their love for all things Fresh.

Modern research has caught up and now consistently supports the theory that people who eat the greatest quantity of fruits and vegetables are about half as likely to develop cancer or many other modern diseases as those who eat little or no fresh fruits and vegetables. In fact, the phytochemicals in whole fruit and vegetables hold the keys to preventing heart disease and other debilitating conditions such as asthma, arthritis, diabetes, and allergies. Still, even the most disciplined person can find it difficult to eat all those raw fruits and vegetables. Juicing plays a major role in ensuring a healthy diet by making it easier to consume the recommended five to eight daily servings of fruits and vegetables.

THE EIGHT BENEFITS OF JUICING

Hydration
Our cells consist mostly of water, which is essential to their proper functioning. That's why our bodies require at least eight glasses of water a day. Raw juice supplies the water you need to replenish lost fluid while providing all the necessary vitamins, minerals, enzymes, and phytochemicals. Juices also promote the alkalinity of body fluids, which is vital for proper immune and metabolic function.

Cleansing
Raw juice has a laxative effect on the body, which helps rid it of toxins. Cleansing the system makes your metabolism more efficient.

Enzymes
Enzymes are the living force present in all living plants. They are most readily available to the body when raw fresh juices are consumed. This life force is a vital quality that is lost in processing, pasteurization, and concentrates.

Sugars
Natural sugars deliver the same energy as pastries, candy, and soft drinks without the chemicals, empty calories, and fats.

Assimilation

Nutrients can be taken into the cells of the body within 15 minutes (as compared with 1 hour or more for nutrients to be assimilated from ingredients with the pulp intact). This saves the energy required for digestion and allows the body to rest while detoxifying or cleansing, before or after physical activity or while recovering from illness.

Chlorophyll

Found only in plants, chlorophyll has a unique structure that allows it to enhance the body's ability to produce hemoglobin, which in turn enhances the delivery of oxygen to the cells.

Antioxidants

Herbs, fruits, and vegetables are high in antioxidants, which counteract the free radicals that can cause cellular damage, aging, and susceptibility to cancers. Top common antioxidant fruits and vegetables include pomegranate, berries, cherries, apples, red beans, kale, red potato, and artichokes.

Pleasure

Making juice at home is fun. It's an interactive activity for couples, roommates, kids, and parents. The fun begins with dreaming up combinations, going shopping for your juicing adventure, prepping and juicing at home, and finally drinking your delicious creations. Drinking freshly squeezed juices and smoothies is a pleasure for the taste buds, and knowing you have just done something for yourself and your loved ones is a pleasure for everyone.

Be sure to incorporate your juices into a well-balanced high-fibre whole food diet. Extracted juices should not completely replace whole fruits and vegetables, since their fibre is also important for eliminating toxins and preventing some forms of cancer.

The Juicing Kitchen

BASIC EQUIPMENT

All you need is a clean cutting board, a good, sharp knife, a tall glass or two smaller glasses, a decent home juicer, and a blender. Some recipes may require only a juicer or a blender, and some may require both.

Juice extractors

A juice extractor separates the nutrients and water contained in fruits, vegetables, and herbs from the pulp or indigestible fibre. There are two basic types of juice extractors: masticating and centrifugal.

Masticating

A masticating juice extractor squeezes the fruits and vegetables through gears, which crush and force them through a fine stainless steel strainer. It takes more time to produce a glass of juice, but the process generates less heat and friction, and so more enzymes are preserved. Plus, it is very quiet.

Centrifugal

In a centrifugal juicer, a spinning basket shreds the fruits and vegetables and forces the juice through a fine stainless steel strainer. Depending on the make of the juicer, pulp can be continuously extracted or collected in the basket. Centrifugal juices cause slight oxidation of the nutrients, but they are much faster and more convenient to use than masticating juicers.

Blenders and food processors

There are some fruits, especially soft fruits and berries, that do not juice well and so, in addition to a juice extractor, it is useful to have a blender or food processor. It enables you to make smoothies and shakes with certain ingredients that were simply never meant to be juiced—nuts, seeds, oils, wheat germ, bee pollen, dried fruits, and herbs. A blender is also essential if you are mixing supplements, protein, and fine green powders into your drinks.

Vitamix blender

A Vitamix blender is the best type for making smoothies and shakes, since it reduces ingredients to a smooth consistency very quickly.

INGREDIENTS

Try to use local and, if possible, organic ingredients, for freshness and to reduce the carbon footprint of whatever you are preparing.

If possible, use grade B maple syrup. Grade B is the darkest and least processed of the maple syrups and arguably the most nutritious. Grade A maple syrup is easy to get at grocery stores, while grade B is generally only available at your local health food store.

Hard ingredients

Juice hard ingredients such as carrots, apples, ginger, and beets in a juicer. Pineapples can be blended, but we juice them to create a liquid base for our shakes and smoothies.

Soft ingredients

Blend soft ingredients such as berries, kiwis, mangoes, papayas, passion fruit, and bananas in a blender.

Broccoli and spinach can be juiced, but we also blend them into our smoothies.

Bananas

You will notice that we love to use bananas in our smoothies. Although we don't use frozen bananas at the Fresh restaurants, I highly recommend using them at home. They will add creaminess and thickness to your drinks as if you added ice cream. Buy plenty of bananas, let them ripen, peel them, and store them in zip-lock bags in the freezer. You will never have to throw away over-ripened bananas again, and you will find your smoothies are colder, creamier, and thicker.

Juice as an ingredient

Most blended drinks call for some juice, and I believe that freshly extracted juice is best. However, it is not essential, and natural, unsweetened, non-concentrate bottled juices, available in many grocery and health food stores, can be used instead.

Avoid juices made from concentrate, which has been boiled and homogenized. This mixture is then frozen and shipped to distributors, where it is defrosted, reconstituted with tap water (generally), and enhanced with flavour and aroma. The concentration process dramatically affects the nutritional value and taste of the juice. At Fresh we never use concentrates.

PREPPING FRUITS AND VEGETABLES

Use common sense when prepping fruits and vegetables for juicing or blending. Generally, if you would peel and pit a fruit or vegetable to eat it whole or cook with, you're going to do that before juicing or blending too. Pears and apples do not need to be cored when using a centrifugal juicer. Citrus fruits can be peeled and juiced or cut in half and squeezed with a citrus press.

The beverage recipes that follow all yield one regular serving (enough to fill a tall glass) or two smaller servings.

Remember: sharing is caring!

Cleanses

The goal of cleansing, detoxifying, or fasting is to release and eliminate toxins stored in the colon and fat cells. These toxins re-enter the bloodstream and circulate in the body. That is why the beginning of a cleansing regimen, juice fast, or detoxifying program is usually accompanied by headaches and some irritability. But don't worry, within a day or two you will be feeling so much better you won't want to stop. Consistency is more important than the length of the cleanse, so try to cleanse once a week, or once a month, or once every three months (you get the idea), for up to three days at a time.

A simple cleanse for me these days can consist of a restricted diet of just vegetable soups, or just fresh juices and raw salads and herbal teas. After years of 21-day juice fasts, master cleansers, and extremely restrictive detox programs, I no longer feel the need to prove to myself that I can do it. I prefer a gentle cleanse every once in a while when I really need it. But because I have established a balanced approach to health and well-being, based on my experience of what makes *me* feel best, I rarely find I need to do anything other than reduce my stress, exercise, get enough rest, drink juice and plenty of water, and eat healthily.

While cleansing, remember that it is important to drink 8 to 10 glasses of water each day to flush the toxins quickly out of your body. Abstaining from alcohol, caffeine, sugar, salt, refined foods, animal products, and fried foods is also key.

These days, I no longer place much importance on whether water used in my drinks is filtered or not. At Fresh we use filtered water, but at home, I am quite comfortable drinking tap water. Which you choose is entirely up to you.

The three cleanses described that follow can be taken individually or in combination with each other. As I am hugely resistant to monotony of any kind, I created the companion cleansers to the Master Cleanser.

If possible, use grade B maple syrup. Grade B is the darkest and least processed of the maple syrups, and arguably the most nutritious. Grade A maple syrup is easy to get at grocery stores, while grade B is generally only available at your local health food store.

Master Cleanser

2	lemons, squeezed
8 oz	water
2 tbsp	maple syrup
dash	cayenne pepper

1. Combine all ingredients in a tall glass. Stir and drink.

Cactus Cleanser

4	limes, squeezed
8 oz	water
2 tbsp	raw agave nectar
dash	cayenne pepper

1. Combine all ingredients in a tall glass. Stir and drink.

Honey Ginger Cleanser

2	lemons, squeezed
1	1-inch piece ginger, sliced
8 oz	water
2 tbsp	unfiltered raw honey
dash	cayenne pepper

1. Combine all ingredients in a tall glass. Stir and drink.

E3Live + Wheatgrass Smoothies

For many years, wheatgrass has been the chlorophyll shot of choice offered at juice bars across North America. Fresh-sprouted wheatgrass provides a quick and extreme fix for those looking to cleanse their blood, liver, and kidneys. That is the upside; the downside is that the intense detoxification and cleansing properties often produce a woozy, nauseous, and unpleasant reaction in first-timers because of the speedy release of toxins from the kidneys and liver into the bloodstream.

The taste can be a challenge too. I liken it to mowing the lawn with your mouth, and many people just cannot stomach the taste or smell of wheatgrass. The solution is to combine shots of wheatgrass with fruity shakes containing pineapple, orange, mint, or mango. You'll find recipes for delicious fruity shakes like these in our previous cookbook, *refresh*.

If you are one of those people who doesn't enjoy drinking wheatgrass and as a result are missing out on its benefits, give E3Live a try. E3Live is an up-and-coming ingredient on the juice bar circuit. It's a beautiful bright green colour, has a milder flavour than wheatgrass, and evokes a gentler reaction in the body. E3Live (Original) and other related E3 products are now widely available in the freezer sections of health food stores across North America. Thaw and store it in the refrigerator, to use in smoothies over the course of a week to 10 days.

E3Live is a raw, wild-harvested, fresh-frozen aquabotanical. It provides 64 easily absorbed vitamins, minerals, and enzymes. It is an extremely nutrient-dense superfood. E3Live has naturally occurring green, blue, and magenta pigments, which reflect the presence of fresh chlorophyll, PEA (the love molecule found in chocolate), phycocyanin, beta carotene, and other unique nutritional factors. PEA acts on the limbic system, which is the emotional centre of the brain. Wheatgrass or spirulina are good substitutes for E3Live in any of these smoothies.

Cosmic Trigger

4	slices pineapple
3	oranges
3 oz	water
1	frozen banana
4	fresh or frozen raspberries
1 oz	E3Live
	ice (optional)

1. Juice the pineapple. Add oranges and water to the juicer to flush the pineapple juice through. Transfer the juice mixture to a blender and add remaining ingredients. Blend, starting on a low setting and then switching to a higher setting, for about 1 minute. Serve in a tall glass.

Tropical Transfusion

4	slices pineapple
3 oz	water
1	frozen banana
4 oz	unsweetened coconut milk
4	fresh or frozen strawberries
1 oz	E3Live
	ice (optional)

1. Juice the pineapple. Add the water to the juicer to flush the juice through. Transfer the juice mixture to a blender and add remaining ingredients. Blend, starting on a low setting and then switching to a higher setting, for about 1 minute. Serve in a tall glass.

Depth Charger

1	½-inch piece ginger
3	pears
3	red apples
½	lemon
1	frozen banana
1 oz	E3Live
	ice (optional)

1. Juice the ginger, followed by the pears, apples, and lemon. Transfer the juice to a blender and add remaining ingredients. Blend, starting on a low setting and then switching to a higher setting, for about 1 minute. Serve in a tall glass.

La Luna

This smoothie is served at La Luna in Nosara, on the Nicoya Peninsula of Costa Rica. It complements E3Live perfectly. La Luna is a Mediterranean-inspired restaurant right on the beach and backed by lush, tropical jungle, complete with howler monkeys and green iguanas. Run by the lovely green-eyed beauty Angelina Fraser, it is another one of those spots that inspires you to sell all your possessions, buy land, and open a little restaurant of your own.

4	oranges
1	mango
1	passion fruit
½	papaya
1 tsp	honey
1 oz	E3Live
	ice (optional)

1. Juice the oranges. Transfer the juice to a blender and add remaining ingredients. Blend, starting on a low setting and then switching to a higher setting, for about 1 minute. Serve in a tall glass.

Fresh & Greens+

In 1995 I discovered greens+ in a tiny store on Church Street in Toronto called Supplements Plus. Church Street was then and still is a centre of activity for the gay community in this city. At that time, the whole world was struggling with the AIDS epidemic. Boosting the immune system was on everyone's minds.

I approached Stewart Brown of Supplements Plus to see if the store would sell greens+ to me at a wholesale cost, so I could include it in some of the juices at Juice for Life. He agreed to, and several tasty combinations were created that worked well as a backdrop to the potent powder. We became the first juice bar to include greens+, along with other supplements such as spirulina, and herbal tinctures such as echinacea, in our shakes and smoothies. This began a long-standing friendship and alliance with Stewart Brown. At Juice for Life, we gave people a chance to try these amazing supplements, to see how good they could feel and to inspire them to make their own fantastic combinations at home.

Through the 1990s, I was a fixture at many AIDS fundraising events, juicing and making greens+ shakes and smoothies. In 1999, when we were about to publish our first cookbook, *Juice for Life: Modern Food and Luscious Juice,* Stewart brought Sam Graci, the creator of greens+, to Fresh on Bloor. Sam had graciously agreed to write the foreword to our book. Accompanying Sam was my hero, Harvey Diamond, who co-wrote the life-changing book *Fit for Life,* about proper food combining. Harvey and Sam were a dynamic duo, full of kind words of encouragement during those early years of building the business in Toronto.

Over time, we got the word out and reinforced the notion that we all could be much better informed and more proactive about our health and well-being. We printed many flyers highlighting the benefits of specific ingredients, including fruits, vegetables, herbs, and spices, until we found ourselves serving a much more educated and savvy customer. Today we learn just as much from our customers and staff as they learn from us. And, at long last, juice bars across the continent now boost their shakes and smoothies with leading-edge supplements, including greens+.

THE BENEFITS OF GREENS+

Greens+ is an award-winning green food supplement containing a unique blend of 23 plant-based ingredients, sea vegetables, enzymes, and probiotic cultures. Although all of these ingredients are superfoods in their own right, it is the synergy of the ingredients in the formula that enhances health and well-being, providing the body with a huge range of beneficial nutrients, phytonutrients, and antioxidants.

Founder Sam Graci developed the greens+ formula over seven years, not with the intention of developing a marketable product but as an extension of his beliefs and personal philosophy on nutrition and lifestyle. He sought to make the benefits of extraordinary superfoods from land and sea available to everyone. His commitment to helping people live healthier lives led to his partnership with Stewart Brown, through which he was able to make the product available to consumers in an economical and convenient way.

Not only does the research behind greens+ make it unique but the formula itself stands apart from other green foods, in my opinion. The specific standardized herbal blend (including Siberian ginseng, licorice, and milk thistle) promotes energy, mental well-being, and overall vitality. The phosphatide complex, including lecithin, enhances the absorption of both fat- and water-soluble nutrients and antioxidants, which contribute to cardiovascular health and provide nerve support for a healthy mental outlook and cognitive function. Greens+ contains the antioxidant equivalent of six servings of organic fruits and vegetables. It also increases alkalinity in the body. A more alkaline body equals a healthier body.

Enjoying the taste of something that is also good for you is the key to having it again and again. On the following pages are five great greens+ cocktails you can enjoy at home. But honestly, folks, you don't need me to create greens+ cocktails for you. The truth is that the powder has a pleasant mild flavour that won't dominate the flavour of your favourite smoothie. You will barely notice it beyond the lovely green hue it brings to your juice. So don't be shy to add it to whatever you are drinking, even if it is just a glass of cold apple juice!

I recommend using 1 tsp greens+ powder at first to get used to the taste, gradually increasing the amount to 1 or 2 tbsp per cocktail.

Super Energy Cocktail

This cocktail has been a well-loved fixture on our menus for many years and has consistently ranked in the top three best-selling juices. You will find it to be highly refreshing, light, and invigorating.

1	1-inch piece ginger
4	slices pineapple
2	red apples
¼	cucumber
1 tsp	greens+ powder
	ice (optional)

1. Juice the ginger, followed by the pineapple, apples, and cucumber. Transfer the juice to a blender and add greens+ and ice. Blend to combine. Serve in a tall glass.

Herbal Ecstasy

This is another extremely refreshing cocktail. The triad of mint, lime, and pear elevate this drink to an entirely new level of thirst quenching.

1	1-inch piece ginger
4	pears
1	lime
1	handful fresh mint
1 tsp	agave nectar
1 tsp	greens+ powder
	ice (optional)

1. Juice the ginger, followed by the pears and lime. Transfer the juice to a blender and add remaining ingredients. Blend to combine. Serve in a tall glass.

Woman's Roar

This is another recipe from the old days that has stood the test of time. Women enjoy it for the iron-rich benefits of the beets, along with the energy surge from the greens+. The apple juice keeps the Woman's Roar from getting too heavy in taste and texture.

1	1-inch piece ginger
4	medium carrots
2	small beets
2	red apples
1 tsp	greens+ powder
	ice (optional)

1. Juice the ginger, followed by the carrots, beets, and apples. Transfer the juice to a blender and add greens+ and ice. Blend to combine. Serve in a tall glass.

Lovers Rock

Simply put, I love Sade and I adore her song "Lovers Rock." The combination of the ingredients in this cocktail remind me of her smooth voice and the sensual nature of the song.

3	oranges
2	grapefruit
2	peaches
4	fresh or frozen strawberries
1 tsp	greens+ powder
	ice (optional)

1. Juice the oranges and grapefruit. Transfer the juice to a blender and add remaining ingredients. Blend to combine. Serve in a tall glass.

Apple Mint Lassi

Have you noticed the massive number of yogurts available these days? It's not surprising, when you consider the many health benefits yogurt offers. Our bodies need a healthy amount of "good" bacteria in the digestive tract, and many yogurts are made using active, good bacteria. One of the words that keeps cropping up around yogurt is "probiotics." Probiotic means "for life" and refers to the living organisms that become good bacteria in the intestinal tract. So when buying yogurt, be sure the label says "live and active cultures." Yogurt is an animal by-product high in protein—about 9 grams per 6-ounce serving. It is also a source of other nutrients, including calcium, vitamins B2 and B12, potassium, and magnesium.

4	red apples
1	lemon
¼	cucumber
1	handful fresh mint
1	handful spinach
2 tbsp	unflavoured yogurt
1 tsp	greens+ powder
	ice (optional)

1. Juice the apples, lemon, and cucumber. Transfer the juice to a blender and add remaining ingredients. Blend to combine. Serve in a tall glass.

Power Shakes

Generally thicker than our smoothies, the power shakes at Fresh combine all sorts of ingredients, including our fresh juices, milks, natural sweeteners, spices, nut butters, grains, exotic fruits, berries, powders, and supplements. They are designed to fill you up with nutritious goodness. They'll refuel your body with the power it needs to enjoy your active life.

Shamrock

Despite the Irish reference, this shake has Japanese roots: matcha—green tea ground into a precious fine powder—is the star ingredient. Other varieties of green tea are grown around the world, but matcha is unique to Japan. It has been at the heart of the traditional Japanese tea ceremony for hundreds of years. The health benefits of matcha exceed those of other green teas because the whole leaf is ingested, not just the brewed water. One glass is equal, in terms of nutritional value and caffeine, to 10 cups of brewed green tea. Matcha is rich in nutrients, antioxidants, and fibre. The chlorophyll and amino acids give matcha its green colour and astringent vegetal taste. But the taste is difficult to describe. To me, it has a complex, bittersweet, rich and addictive flavour.

1	frozen banana
10	drops pure peppermint oil
8 oz	unsweetened, unflavoured soy milk
1 tsp	matcha
1 tsp	agave nectar

1. Place all the ingredients in a blender. Blend, starting on a low setting and then switching to a higher setting, for about 1 minute. Serve in a tall glass.

Surfo

Here's another hip Spanish beach slang term for you (useful in case you ever find yourself wanting to impress a hot girl or guy on the beach in Mexico). A "surfo" is someone who surfs and, let me tell you, surfers love their smoothies more than anyone. I am not a surfer, but I like having this combination anyway before a power walk or yoga class.

1	guava
1	kiwi
1	frozen banana
8 oz	unsweetened, unflavoured soy milk
4	fresh or frozen strawberries
1 tbsp	vanilla-flavoured protein powder
	ice (optional)

1. Place all the ingredients in a blender. Blend, starting on a low setting and then switching to a higher setting, for about 1 minute. Serve in a tall glass.

Pomegranate Açai

The power in this shake is derived from the triple threat of antioxidant-rich ingredients: cherries, pomegranate, and açai berries. I have added mango juice for its natural lingering sweetness. Add a vanilla-flavoured protein powder to make this a super-potent and energizing drink to fuel your workout, surf session, or yoga practice. Açai berries, which hail from the jungles of Central and South America, are now widely available in the freezer section of most health food stores.

8 oz	bottled mango juice
6 oz	bottled pomegranate juice
2 tbsp	frozen açai berries
6	cherries, pitted

1. Place all the ingredients in a blender. Blend, starting on a low setting and then switching to a higher setting, for about 1 minute. Serve in a tall glass.

The Giving Tree

This shake is loaded with calcium-rich almonds and almond milk. I am a huge fan of this delicate-tasting and versatile nut. Originally farmed in countries throughout the Middle East, including Iran, Saudi Arabia, Israel, Lebanon, and Syria, almonds are a valuable source of vitamin E, phosphorous, iron, magnesium, zinc, selenium, copper, and niacin. Almonds also have a very high concentration of folate (folic acid) and are an important dietary staple for pregnant women, as well as for women trying to get pregnant. One cup of raw almonds has 12 percent of the recommended daily allowance of folic acid. If you don't have almond butter, you can simply throw a handful of raw almonds into the blender for the same result.

1	frozen banana
8 oz	unsweetened, unflavoured almond milk
4	fresh or frozen strawberries
1 tbsp	almond butter
1 tsp	agave nectar
	ice (optional)

1. Place all the ingredients in a blender. Blend, starting on a low setting and then switching to a higher setting, for about 1 minute. Serve in a tall glass.

Miles Davis

Miles Davis is the name of my new super-duper scooter in Mexico. For the Aztecs, amaranth was known as a superfood. They believed it had magical properties and gave it to hunters and runners for sustained energy. Amaranth is a good source of protein and is rich in the amino acids, with the highest lysine content of any grain. Pound for pound, amaranth has triple the amount of fibre of wheat, and it has more than 20 percent of the recommended daily amount of calcium, iron, magnesium, and folate. Finally, amaranth is also a good source of potassium, phosphorous, and vitamins A, C, and E. Rice or soy milk also work well in this shake.

1	frozen banana
8 oz	unsweetened, unflavoured almond milk
4	fresh or frozen raspberries
2 tbsp	amaranth
4	dates, pitted
	ice (optional)

1. Place all the ingredients in a blender. Blend, starting on a low setting and then switching to a higher setting, for about 1 minute. Serve in a tall glass.

Fruity Green

Broccoli has gotten a bad reputation among kids and even many grown-ups as one of the most dreaded vegetables. Could be because it's a member of the brassica family, which includes cauliflower, cabbage, and Brussels sprouts, and which all have a strong and sulphurous flavour. Being a lover of broccoli, I set out to see if I could find a delicious way to sneak this highly nutritious yet unloved vegetable into our customers' tummies. I discovered that juicing or cooking broccoli accentuates its strong taste. Taking a risk, I threw it raw into the blender, and was delighted to find that blending it with other fruits and vegetables hides its flavours. Feeling brazen and subversive, I reached for raw spinach, the second-most unloved vegetable after broccoli, and found that my fruity concoction hid that too.

Broccoli is high in vitamin C, which aids iron absorption in the body. It is also rich in fibre and contains a good amount of folic acid, potassium, and calcium. Spinach is a very nutrient-dense food and an excellent source of vitamins A, E, K, C, B2, and B6. It also provides magnesium, folate, iron, calcium, zinc, potassium, and even omaga-3 fatty acids.

4	slices pineapple
2	oranges
3 oz	water
8 oz	bottled mango juice
4	florets broccoli
1	handful spinach
1	frozen banana
	ice (optional)

1. Juice the pineapple. Add the oranges and water to the juicer to flush the pineapple juice through. Transfer the juice mixture to a blender and add remaining ingredients. Blend, starting on a low setting and then switching to a higher setting, for about 1 minute. Serve in a tall glass.

Wild Bull

The "wild bull" here is found in the double dose of ginseng and royal jelly. Ginseng is a known stimulant and has long been used in China as an aphrodisiac. I cannot personally attest to its latter quality, but who am I to argue with a nation of a billion people? Ginseng is an adaptogen, which means it increases resistance to fatigue, stress, trauma, and anxiety, without creating side effects, even when taken in extra-large doses. Royal jelly is produced in beehives for the nourishment of the queen bee. The vitamin B and protein content in royal jelly is very high. Royal jelly is readily available in health food stores and in Chinatown. It contains 17 amino acids, including all eight essential amino acids.

4	oranges
1	frozen banana
1	vial royal jelly
1	vial ginseng
4	fresh or frozen strawberries
	ice (optional)

1. Juice the oranges. Transfer the juice to a blender and add remaining ingredients. Blend, starting on a low setting and then switching to a higher setting, for about 1 minute. Serve in a tall glass.

Chidito

Chidito is the diminutive in Spanish slang for "cool." This heavenly combination was created especially for Guadua, my favourite restaurant and beach lounge in Puerto Escondido, Oaxaca, on the Pacific coast of Mexico. This stunning, breezy, bamboo, vegetarian-friendly restaurant sits on a wild stretch of beach, just 5 minutes from the famous surf break, the MexiPipe. Diego, Ricardo, and Moises, the three coolest guys you'll ever meet, sold all their belongings, packed up their lives in Mexico City, and moved to Puerto Escondido to live their dream. As a fellow restaurateur, I have big respect for the risk they took and for what they have achieved through their hard work and perseverance.

1	frozen banana
8 oz	bottled mango juice
8 oz	unsweetened, unflavoured soy milk
2 tbsp	fresh or frozen blueberries
1 tbsp	vanilla-flavoured protein powder
1 tsp	agave nectar
	ice (optional)

1. Place all the ingredients in a blender. Blend, starting on a low setting and then switching to a higher setting, for about 1 minute. Serve in a tall glass.

Chi-Spa

Chia seed is a nutritious superfood that's making a big comeback these days. It used to be a common crop centuries ago but then was nearly forgotten. Grown and harvested in southern Mexico, the seeds are now available in most health food stores in North America. This tiny super seed was a staple of the Indians of the Southwest and Mexico. Known as the "running food," its use for high-energy endurance has been recorded as far back as the Aztecs. It was said the Aztec warriors subsisted on chia seed during the conquests.

The chia seed can soak up 10 times its weight in water and is easily digestible. When inside your body, the seeds help you stay hydrated longer and retain electrolytes in your body's fluids. Chia seeds provide ample calcium, protein, and omega-3 fatty acids to your tissues. The seeds are also rich in boron, which helps the body assimilate and use calcium.

2	red apples
1	frozen banana
1	1-inch piece ginger, sliced
6 oz	unsweetened, unflavoured soy milk
4	dates, pitted
1 tbsp	chia seeds
dash	cinnamon
	ice (optional)

1. Juice the apples. Transfer the juice to a blender and add remaining ingredients. Blend, starting on a low setting and then switching to a higher setting, for about 1 minute. Serve in a tall glass.

Espresso Shakes

Nothing beats an espresso shake as a way to recharge your batteries and refresh yourself when you need it most. It can be a useful tool to pick you up by your socks or a frivolous luxury when you feel like treating yourself. It all depends on the ingredients in the shake. I like to play around with healthy ingredients like granola or chia seeds, as well as decadent ingredients like chunks of white or dark chocolate.

These days at Fresh, we've been using a new kind of organically grown coffee bean. It's certified bird-friendly, which means that no birds have been harmed nor their habitat destroyed in the production of the bean. Bird-friendly coffee beans are grown on farms under a shady canopy of trees that provides a resting stop for migrating neotropical birds. The clearing of forests for coffee plantations has resulted in habitat loss and caused a decline in migratory songbird populations that winter in the rainforests of Central and South America.

Feel free to use any kind of milk you like in these shakes. All kinds—cow, goat, almond, rice, or hemp—will blend deliciously with the other ingredients. If you are not able to brew espresso, use French press or strong filtered coffee instead. Sometimes for fun I'll even throw a few whole espresso beans into the blender. They add a nice texture and more caffeine. Enjoy your java!

White Tiger

This is a deliciously decadent espresso shake. If you are one of those people with a sweet tooth for white chocolate, this shake is especially for you. Chunks of white baking chocolate work well here.

6	ice cubes
4	chunks white chocolate
1	single or double shot espresso
1	frozen banana
8 oz	unsweetened, unflavoured soy milk
1 tbsp	raw almonds
1 tsp	agave nectar

1. Place all the ingredients in a blender. Blend, starting on a low setting and then switching to a higher setting, for about 1 minute. Serve in a tall glass.

Magnum

This is the Rolls-Royce of espresso shakes.

6	ice cubes
4	chunks dark chocolate
1	single or double shot espresso
1	frozen banana
8 oz	unsweetened, unflavoured soy milk
1 tbsp	raw pecans
1 tsp	agave nectar

1. Place all the ingredients in a blender. Blend, starting on a low setting and then switching to a higher setting, for about 1 minute. Serve in a tall glass.

Orale

O*rale* is Spanish slang for "Let's go!" You can use your favourite granola in this recipe, though I recommend a sugar-free granola that has lots of fruit, nuts, and seeds in it.

6	ice cubes
1	single or double shot espresso
1	frozen banana
8 oz	unsweetened, unflavoured soy milk
2 tbsp	granola
1 tsp	agave nectar
dash	cinnamon

1. Place all the ingredients in a blender. Blend, starting on a low setting and then switching to a higher setting, for about 1 minute. Serve in a tall glass.

Diesel

This espresso shake is loaded with the complex carbohydrates of chia seeds and amaranth, which help metabolize the caffeine gradually in your body.

6	ice cubes
1	frozen banana
1	single or double shot espresso
8 oz	unsweetened, unflavoured soy milk
2 tbsp	chia seeds
1 tbsp	amaranth
1 tsp	agave nectar
dash	cinnamon

1. Place all the ingredients in a blender. Blend, starting on a low setting and then switching to a higher setting, for about 1 minute. Serve in a tall glass.

Avocado Smoothies

A medium-sized avocado contains a whopping 731 calories and more than 30 grams of fat. But this beautiful fruit's nutritional benefits outweigh its negative reputation due to that high caloric content. And for all those lucky individuals wishing to gain weight, avocados can bring healthy fats and calories to your diet. So here's the real skinny on avocados. Avocados contain monounsaturated healthy fats, are high in fibre, and are a perfect food for pregnant women. This creamy, delicious fruit contains over 30 percent of the recommended daily dosage of folic acid and more potassium than bananas.

We like to use pure coconut water as the liquid base for all of our avocado smoothies because it's light, nutritious, and neutral in flavour. Its popularity is rising and it can now be found in many grocery stores and health food stores. Coconut water is also super-hydrating and will balance out the rich and more filling ingredients. Feel free to substitute water, apple juice, or soymilk for the coconut water.

Avocado Banana Spinach

I have always wanted to include avocados in our smoothies, knowing how awesome they are, but I have been too shy to try it, until recently. It turns out our customers were more than ready to embrace this exotic combination. The spinach takes a backseat here, accentuating this smoothie with green goodness.

1	frozen banana
1	handful spinach
½	avocado
10 oz	pure coconut water
	ice (optional)

1. Place all the ingredients in a blender. Blend, starting on a low setting and then switching to a higher setting, for about a minute. Serve in a tall glass.

Avocado Pineapple Basil

Admittedly, avocado, pineapple, and basil are an unlikely trio of star ingredients, but they work magnificently together. This smoothie is bursting with flavour.

3	slices pineapple
1	handful fresh basil, stems and all
½	avocado
½	vanilla bean
10 oz	pure coconut water
	ice (optional)

1. Place all the ingredients in a blender. Blend, starting on a low setting and then switching to a higher setting, for about a minute. Serve in a tall glass.

Avocado Mango Ginger

I discovered this combination of ingredients thanks to a facial I had in a spa in Bali five years ago. I always knew it would be even better as a smoothie!

4	ginger slices
1	mango
½	avocado
10 oz	pure coconut water
1 tsp	flaxseeds
	ice (optional)

1. Place all the ingredients in a blender. Blend, starting on a low setting and then switching to a higher setting, for about a minute. Serve in a tall glass.

Avocado Blueberry Granola

This is an awesome breakfast-on-the-go smoothie. Add 1 tbsp spirulina for an added energy boost to start your day off perfectly.

½	avocado
2 tbsp	fresh or frozen blueberries
2 tbsp	granola
10 oz	pure coconut water
1 tsp	honey
	ice (optional)

1. Place all the ingredients in a blender. Blend, starting on a low setting and then switching to a higher setting, for about a minute. Serve in a tall glass.

Avocado Almond Cacao

This combination has been on my mind for a long time, and I'm happy to finally share it. The cacao beans and dates deliver a natural sweetness to this already highly charged protein-rich smoothie.

4	dates, pitted
½	avocado
10 oz	pure coconut water
1 tbsp	almond butter
1 tbsp	raw cacao beans
	ice (optional)

1. Place all the ingredients in a blender. Blend, starting on a low setting and then switching to a higher setting, for about a minute. Serve in a tall glass.

Avocado Cashew Banana

This smoothie is a vegan dream. There are lots of healthy calories and supreme fuel for your hungry body here.

3	ice cubes
1	frozen banana
½	avocado
10 oz	pure coconut water
2 tbsp	raw cashews

1. Place all the ingredients in a blender. Blend, starting on a low setting and then switching to a higher setting, for about a minute. Serve in a tall glass.

Fruit Smoothies

In the Fresh world, a smoothie is a concoction of blended whole fruit and fruit juices. It does not contain added sugar, dairy, additives, or preservatives and, most importantly, it it's made with fresh juices. We make exceptions only when we cross over to include some vegetables, such as beets or carrots, coconut milk or coconut water, nut butters, spices, natural sweeteners, and "not from concentrate" bottled juices.

Concentrated juice has been boiled and homogenized. This mixture is then frozen and shipped to distributors, where it is defrosted, reconstituted with tap water (generally), and enhanced with flavour and aroma. The concentration process dramatically affects the nutritional value and taste of the juice. At Fresh we never use concentrates.

Ultimately, fresh is best, but there is a good argument for sometimes opting for frozen fruit. Freezing fruit does not make it nutritionally worthless. Freezing is useful because it slows down the growth of bacteria that make fruit ripen and rotten. Freezers can keep food fresh for longer, which allows you to store more so you have it ready when you need it. I prefer to make my smoothies with frozen berries and bananas.

Cherry Blossom

Beautiful cherry blossoms are the flower of the Japanese cherry tree, known as the "sakura." In Japanese culture, the cherry blossom is a symbol of good fortune and is also an emblem of love, affection, and spring. Cherries are one of the first fruits to ripen but have one of the shortest growing seasons. At Fresh we use pitted frozen cherries all year round. Cherries are cherished for their concentration of antioxidants, but they also possess high levels of melatonin, which helps to relax and regulate sleep cycles.

4	red apples
1	frozen banana
6	cherries, pitted
2 tbsp	fresh or frozen raspberries
	ice (optional)

1. Juice the apples. Transfer the juice to a blender and add remaining ingredients. Blend, starting on a low setting and then switching to a higher setting, for about 1 minute. Serve in a tall glass.

Yellow Brick Road

Our customers love combining carrot and orange juice. I took this one step further to create a thick, creamy smoothie that is delicious and filling.

3	medium carrots
3	oranges
1	frozen banana
	ice (optional)

1. Juice the carrots and oranges. Transfer the juice to a blender and add the banana and ice. Blend, starting on a low setting and then switching to a higher setting, for about 1 minute. Serve in a tall glass.

Pink Dolphin

Pink dolphins actually exist, in the Amazon River. This is a very popular smoothie with little kids who get to choose their smoothie all by themselves.

1	frozen banana
8 oz	bottled mango juice
2 tbsp	fresh or frozen raspberries
	ice (optional)

1. Place all the ingredients in a blender. Blend, starting on a low setting and then switching to a higher setting, for about 1 minute. Serve in a tall glass.

Oompa Loompa

Named after the little orange men in the movie *Willy Wonka & the Chocolate Factory*, this popular combination was created a few years ago by Nigel Churcher, who loves a light, refreshing citrus smoothie, with no banana, please! The Oompa Loompa can also be gently warmed in a saucepan for a hot toddy if you are feeling under the weather.

1	½-inch piece ginger
6	slices pineapple
2	pink grapefruit
½	lemon, peeled
	ice (optional)

1. Juice the ginger, followed by the pineapple, grapefruit, and lemon. Transfer the juice to a blender and blend with ice if using. Serve in a tall glass.

Lucky Charm

Unlike the popular kids' sugary cereal of the same name, this smoothie is loaded with vitamin C, anti-oxidants, and all-natural sweetness.

8 oz	bottled mango juice
2 tbsp	fresh or frozen raspberries
4	fresh or frozen strawberries
2 tbsp	fresh or frozen blueberries
	ice (optional)

1. Place all the ingredients in a blender. Blend, starting on a low setting and then switching to a higher setting, for about 1 minute. Serve in a tall glass.

Pebble Beach

I have the fondest memories of sitting at the kitchen table with my dad, peeling pomegranate and painstakingly removing the small ruby seeds from the bitter pith. By now, we probably all know that pomegranate juice contains three times the antioxidants, ounce for ounce, than a glass of red wine or a cup of green tea. But, even better yet, I recently discovered that my beloved pomegranate has over 40 percent of the recommended daily dose of vitamin C. If you are looking for a less-than-sweet smoothie, this one is pleasingly tart, thanks to the pomegranate juice.

1	frozen banana
8 oz	bottled pomegranate juice
4	fresh or frozen strawberries
	ice (optional)

1. Place all the ingredients in a blender. Blend, starting on a low setting and then switching to a higher setting, for about 1 minute. Serve in a tall glass.

Lady Bug

The Lady Bug is a kids' favourite at Fresh. I'm not sure if it's the name that attracts or the combination of ingredients, but it is a big winner. Because this smoothie is banana-free, it is lighter and less filling than those made with bananas.

3	red apples
4	fresh or frozen strawberries
2 tbsp	fresh or frozen blueberries
	ice (optional)

1. Juice the apples. Transfer the juice to a blender and add remaining ingredients. Blend, starting on a low setting and then switching to a higher setting, for about 1 minute. Serve in a tall glass.

Love Your Peaches

Peaches have become the favourite fruit of our summers. They are the largest of all the stone fruits and are packed with nutrition. Peaches are full of vitamin A, which promotes good vision and improves skin health, and vitamin C, known for its immune-boosting benefits. The skin of the peach is also packed with nutrients, so don't peel your peaches, please! Let peaches ripen on the kitchen counter, and use them in smoothies once they are soft. You can easily substitute nectarines for peaches in this smoothie.

2	oranges
8 oz	bottled mango juice
2	peaches, sliced
	ice (optional)

1. Juice the oranges. Transfer juice to a blender and add remaining ingredients. Blend, starting on a low setting and then switching to a higher setting, for about 1 minute. Serve in a tall glass.

Chocolate Monkey

All little monkeys love chocolate, right? This tastes just like a peanut butter and banana sandwich with chocolate. Kids adore this smoothie, and adults secretly do as well. Be sure to choose an all-natural peanut butter with no added ingredients. I like chunky peanut butter for extra texture in this smoothie.

4	red apples
1	frozen banana
2 tbsp	natural peanut butter
1 tbsp	dark cocoa
	ice (optional)

1. Juice the apples. Transfer the juice to a blender and add remaining ingredients. Blend, starting on a low setting and then switching to a higher setting, for about 1 minute. Serve in a tall glass.

Fresh Mojito

This smoothie is so exotic and good for you. The combination of blended fresh mint leaves and lime juice elevates it to a whole new level of light and refreshing. The papaya grounds this drink with nutritional goodness and gives it the sweetness and body it needs.

8	slices pineapple
1	lime
3 oz	water
1	frozen banana
1	handful fresh mint
½	small papaya
dash	agave nectar
	ice (optional)

1. Juice the pineapple and lime. Add the water to the juicer to flush the juice through. Transfer the juice to a blender and add remaining ingredients. Blend, starting on a low setting and then switching to a higher setting, for about 1 minute. Serve in a tall glass.

Jungle Berry

I discovered delicious açai berry smoothies while travelling in Brazil a few years ago. To my delight, it is now widely available in health food stores across North America. The deep purple açai berry is native to the jungles of Central and South America. A relative of blueberries, cranberries, red grapes, and other blue purple fruits, açai berries contain a high concentration of anthocyanins and flavonoids—powerful antioxidants that help defend the body against life's stressors. Antioxidants help protect our bodies' vulnerable cells, reducing the risk of disease and slowing the aging process.

4	red apples
1	frozen banana
3 tbsp	frozen açai berries
	ice (optional)

1. Juice the apples. Transfer the juice to a blender and add remaining ingredients. Blend, starting on a low setting and then switching to a higher setting, for about 1 minute. Serve in a tall glass.

La Punta

I was walking on the beach early one morning when a bronzed, buff Italian surfer around 50 years old emerged smiling from the ocean. As we chatted, he told me that every day without fail he makes this smoothie, to drink before his surf session. This is the perfect early-morning smoothie. The citrus cleanses, the pineapple and papaya improve digestion, and the carrots provide the nutritional building blocks needed to start your day off right.

4	slices pineapple
4	medium carrots
2	oranges
½	papaya, peeled
	ice (optional)

1. Juice the pineapple, carrots, and oranges. Transfer the juice to a blender and add the papaya and ice. Blend, starting on a low setting and then switching to a higher setting, for about 1 minute. Serve in a tall glass.

Modern Vampire

I love watching people's faces when they taste this unusual juice. Complete surprise and delight! Beets contain sodium, magnesium, calcium, iron, and phosphorus. They are also high in carbohydrates and a great instant energy source. Unlike processed foods, which are high in carbohydrates, beets will invigorate your body. Beets can satisfy your hunger and your sweet tooth too.

3	oranges
2	small beets
1	½-inch piece ginger
2 tbsp	fresh or frozen raspberries
	ice (optional)

1. Juice the oranges, beets, and ginger. Transfer the juice to a blender and add the raspberries and ice. Blend, starting on a low setting and then switching to a higher setting, for about 1 minute. Serve in a tall glass.

Mi Amor

Need I say more, *mi amor?*

1	frozen banana
8 oz	bottled mango juice
2 tbsp	fresh or frozen blueberries
2 tbsp	fresh or frozen raspberries
1 tsp	honey
	ice (optional)

1. Place all the ingredients in a blender. Blend, starting on a low setting and then switching to a higher setting, for about 1 minute. Serve in a tall glass.

Vegetable Cocktails

I am always on the lookout for unlikely vegetable combinations, always making the effort to think outside the box so I can come up with unique healthful juices. In this group, the less common ingredients include sweet potato, broccoli, red pepper, fresh mint leaves, limes, and hemp seeds. You can eliminate the need for ice if the vegetables are chilled before juicing. Wash the veggies thoroughly but don't peel the sweet potato, carrots, cucumber, apples, or ginger, as that's where much of the nutrients are.

Gaia

This is named after a beautiful bouncing baby named Gaia, who especially loves these ingredients in her purée. *Gaia* means earth, and I like to thank that Gaia not only for her rivers, mountains, oceans, and blue skies but also for baby Gaia, who has brought so much joy and laughter into my life. The sweet potato and carrots together in this cocktail provide a double punch of beta carotene.

1	½-inch piece ginger
1	handful spinach
½	sweet potato
4	medium carrots
dash	cinnamon

1. Juice the ginger, followed by the spinach, sweet potato, and carrots. Stir in the cinnamon and serve in a tall glass.

Detoxifier

When detoxifying, it's all about the greens. Every self-respecting juice bar should have at least one all-green juice on its menu, in my opinionated opinion. The apples lighten up and sweeten this green juice just enough so you can really enjoy it. Add a squeeze of lemon to lighten it up even more.

6	stalks parsley
1	handful kale
1	handful spinach
3	stalks celery
4	red apples

1. Juice the parsley, kale, and spinach first, followed by the celery and apples. Stir to combine. Serve in a tall glass.

20/20

Red peppers are especially high in vitamin C and also lend a unique smoky flavour to this juice that masks the sulphurous taste of the broccoli.

6	stalks parsley
1	handful spinach
4	florets broccoli
½	red pepper
6	medium carrots

1. Juice the parsley, spinach, and broccoli first, followed by the red pepper and carrots. Stir to combine. Serve in a tall glass.

Carrot Twist

This is easily one of the most common juices at juice bars around the world, and for good reason. It's refreshing and nutritious and sweet.

1	1-inch piece ginger
3	oranges
6	medium carrots

1. Juice the ginger first, followed by the oranges and carrots. Stir to combine. Serve in a tall glass.

Lemonades

During the spring and summer months, we sell gallons of lemonade at Fresh. A healthy, naturally sweetened lemonade prepared with fresh lemons is a great way to hydrate and cleanse your body.

Fresh Lemonade

2	lemons
4	ice cubes
8 oz	water
1 tsp	agave nectar

1. Juice the lemons. Transfer the juice to a blender and add remaining ingredients. Blend for 30 seconds. Serve in a tall glass.

Watermelon Lemonade

6	slices watermelon
2	lemons
1 tsp	honey
4	ice cubes

1. Juice the watermelon and lemons. Transfer the juice to a blender and add the honey and ice. Blend for 30 seconds. Serve in a tall glass.

Ginger Lemonade

4	slices ginger
2	lemons
4	ice cubes
8 oz	water
1 tsp	agave nectar

1. Juice the ginger, followed by the lemons. Transfer the juice to a blender and add remaining ingredients. Blend for 30 seconds. Serve in a tall glass.

Orange Mint Lemonade

2	oranges
2	lemons
4	ice cubes
1	handful fresh mint
6 oz	water
1 tsp	honey

1. Juice the oranges, followed by the lemons. Transfer the juice to a blender and add remaining ingredients. Blend for 30 seconds. Serve in a tall glass.

Cool Cuke

You can never go wrong with apple, mint, and lime. Adding the cucumber elevates this juice to a hydrating, rejuvenating, and beauty-boosting cocktail.

1	handful fresh mint
1	lime
¼	cucumber
4	red apples

1. Juice the mint, lime, and cucumber first, followed by the apples. Stir to combine. Serve in a tall glass.

Apple Hemp

I was going to call this the "Waldorf" because it tastes just like a Waldorf salad. Hemp seeds add a rich but subtle nutty accent.

6	stalks parsley
3	stalks celery
3	red apples
1	lemon
1 tbsp	hulled hemp seeds

1. Juice the parsley, celery, and apples, followed by the lemon. Transfer the juice to a blender and add the hemp seeds. Serve in a tall glass.

Index